rer   Jt

Theodore Roosevelt
and the Idea of Race

THEODORE ROOSEVELT
and the Idea of Race

THOMAS G. DYER

Louisiana State University Press
Baton Rouge and London

Copyright © 1980 by Louisiana State University Press
Manufactured in the United States of America

Design: Albert Crochet
Typeface: VIP Caledonia
Composition: LSU Press
Printing: Thomson-Shore, Inc.
Binding: John Dekker & Sons, Inc.

LIBRARY OF CONGRESS CATALOGING IN PUBLICATION DATA

Dyer, Thomas G
    Theodore Roosevelt and the idea of race.

    Bibliography: p.
    Includes index.
    1.   Roosevelt, Theodore, Pres. U.S., 1858–1919—Views
on race.   2.   Race.   I.   Title.
E757.D9   301.45'1'0973   79–20151
ISBN 0–8071–0658–5

For Anna and Our Parents

Contents

	Acknowledgments	ix
	Introduction	xi
I	The Racial Education of Theodore Roosevelt	1
II	Theory	21
III	History and the Anglo-Saxon Tradition	45
IV	Indians	69
V	Blacks	89
VI	Race, Immigration, and Imperialism	123
VII	Race Suicide	143
	Conclusion	168
	Bibliography	171
	Index	177

Acknowledgments

In the broadest sense, this book is an attempt to illuminate the racial thinking of Progressive Era Americans and by implication to point to the startling vestiges of those earlier racial ideas in both popular and formal contemporary thought. The instruction that I received in various seminars in American intellectual history and black history under Professor Charles Crowe of the University of Georgia greatly expanded my awareness of the pervasiveness of racism in American society and in particular the importance of Progressive Era racial thought to the development of later racial theory and race relations. If this book possesses any merit, much of the credit belongs to Professor Crowe.

My debts extend much farther, however. I am particularly indebted to Numan V. Bartley for sage advice and counsel rendered during many late afternoon conferences. Lester D. Stephens and F. N. Boney of the University of Georgia read the manuscript and offered very useful suggestions, as did Willard Gatewood of the University of Arkansas and Idus A. Newby of the University of Hawaii. I am deeply obligated to all of them.

Graduate school colleagues James C. Cobb, James M. Gifford, Clarence L. Mohr, Tennant S. McWilliams, and Von V. Pittman made graduate history study at the University of Georgia exciting and memorable. My ideas were largely shaped in seminars in which they were participants and I owe them a great deal. Ward Lewis of the Department of Germanic and Slavic Languages, the University of Georgia, translated the material from the *Nibelungenlied* and introduced me to some of the mysteries of Middle High German.

The Institute of Higher Education, the University of Georgia, provided extremely valuable support during the revision of the manuscript. I am especially grateful to Cameron L. Fincher, director, for the understanding and advice he gave a junior colleague. Nancy Szypulski, Patty Swain, Cindy Houser, and Lynne Chandler skillfully typed the manuscript, while Mary Snyder facilitated production of the final draft in a number of ways.

My greatest obligations are to the members of my family to whom this book is dedicated. My parents-in-law, John and Elizabeth Barnes, gave constant encouragement. My parents, I. G. and Nina C. Dyer, provided years of patience, fortitude, and high example which can never be adequately acknowledged. Finally, I owe the largest debt to my wife, Anna Burns Dyer, whose unflagging good humor and devotion saw us both through to the completion of the project.

Introduction

In focusing on the mind of Theodore Roosevelt, this book explores the dimensions of race thinking at the turn of the century. Although the study seeks to suggest ways in which the idea of race affected Roosevelt and influenced his political career, its primary purpose is to demonstrate the importance of race thinking during the period by accentuating the development and scope of the race idea in the mind of one individual. Roosevelt is an apt subject for such an analysis because of the extent of his intellectual activity and because he regularly expressed himself on virtually any subject which interested him. Thus, it is Roosevelt the race thinker, not Roosevelt the politician who occupies center stage.

Theodore Roosevelt and the Idea of Race also seeks to explore a number of specific questions. In what proportions do popular thought and formal racial theory appear in Roosevelt's thought? In what intellectual context did his racial speculations take place? How was his racial thought related to broader areas of intellectual activity such as natural science and social philosophy? How did Roosevelt regard various white and nonwhite ethnic groups? Did he accept tenets of "pseudo-scientific" racial thought? How did he reconcile American democratic ideals with the reality of a caste society based upon race? How did Roosevelt's racial thought conform to the prevailing philosophies of the late nineteenth and early twentieth centuries? Did he regard racial characteristics as permanent and unchangeable or did he stress mutability? What functions did the idea of race perform in Roosevelt's world view? How did Roosevelt regard racial intermixture? Were sex and race related in his thought? While it may not be possible to respond to each of these questions exhaustively, some answers to each will be suggested.

One of the assumptions of this study has been that investigation of how the idea of race operated at the turn of the century can be profitably approached by looking at an individual idea system rather than cataloging the isolated and often unrelated thoughts of a number of thinkers. Therefore the study emphasizes the dynamic quality of Roosevelt's race thinking by observing the interaction of the components of the race idea. At the same time it is here assumed that ideas are discrete entities which the historian may analyze and that analysis of formal ideas may be enhanced by attention to the nontheoretical aspects of thought. To this end care has been given to the popular aspects of Roosevelt's race thinking and to the jargon in which he often expressed these ideas. This entails attention to language as the raw material of ideas and observations of change or special emphasis in language which may offer clues to change in ideation. The study also assumes that ideas are a form of behavior never completely divorced from the realm of "action" and that Roosevelt's ideas must be regarded as active elements of his experience rather than as passive reflectors of a "climate of opinion."

While much has been written about Roosevelt's presidential policies and how they affected various racial groups, historians have neither explored the complexity and variety of his racial opinions nor investigated the importance of race in his world view. Scholars have largely contented themselves with discussion of whether Roosevelt was a racist, a debate which has yielded little new about Roosevelt or about the character of race thinking and its impact on American life.[1] For example, William Harbaugh, one of Roosevelt's biographers, has declared that "because Roosevelt used the terms *race* and *na-*

1. From a purely technical standpoint, Roosevelt and his contemporaries could not have thought of themselves as "racists," since the word had not yet entered the language and would not until after the late 1930s. I use the word *racist* here as synonomous with one who practices race prejudice and race discrimination—both terms which came into usage during Roosevelt's lifetime.

tion interchangeably, many of his harsh judgments about ethnic groups have been incorrectly characterized as racist."[2] Similarly, in a study of the racial attitudes of American presidents
from Lincoln to Theodore Roosevelt, George Sinkler obscurely
concluded that "while most of the Presidents of this period
were not racists (though a case might be made against Roosevelt) in the full sense of the word, the term was useful [for
Sinkler] because much of the thought of the period took just
that form."[3]

While Harbaugh and Sinkler appear to minimize the racist
quality of Roosevelt's thought, other scholars have displayed
far less doubt about the character of Rooseveltian racial theory.
Perhaps the harshest assessment of Roosevelt as race thinker
came from the sociologist Pierre L. van den Berghe, who placed
Roosevelt in very select company when he wrote: "Western
racism had its poets like Kipling, its philosophers like Gobineau
and Chamberlain, its statesmen like Hitler, Theodore Roosevelt, and Verwoerd." For van den Berghe, Roosevelt, in the
final analysis, was a "virulent bigot" and a "lesser luminary"
as a race theorist who properly belonged in the category of
such race thinkers as Adolf Hitler, Madison Grant, and Charles
Carroll. Despite van den Berghe's failure to document these
claims and despite his apparent lack of familiarity with early-
twentieth-century race theory, his views of Roosevelt may more
accurately reflect the dominant scholarly image of Roosevelt
as racist than the opinions of Harbaugh and Sinkler.[4] In view of
this disagreement and confusion about the character of Roosevelt's racial ideology, this study seeks to clarify some of the issues by viewing TR's racial theory as an integrated whole.

2. William Harbaugh (ed.), *The Writings of Theodore Roosevelt* (Indianapolis
and New York, 1967), 197–200.
3. George Sinkler, *The Racial Attitudes of American Presidents from Abraham
Lincoln to Theodore Roosevelt* (New York, 1972), 3–4.
4. Pierre L. van den Berghe, *Race and Racism* (New York, 1967), 13, 16, 87, 94.

Theodore Roosevelt
and the Idea of Race

CHAPTER I

The Racial Education
of Theodore Roosevelt

From the mid–nineteenth century through the first three decades of the twentieth, racial ideologies became an increasingly influential force in American life. During this time popular thought and public policy leaned heavily upon formal racial
theories as white Americans defined roles of inferiority for nonwhites and ethnics whose appearances and traits relegated
them to low social and political status. For blacks, Orientals,
and Indians, the surge of racist thought and policy brought systematic exclusion from the American polity while other groups,
including Latins and eastern and southern Europeans, encountered a thicket of laws and customs which effectively barred
them from full participation in American life.

Theodore Roosevelt's life ran concurrently with this efflorescence of laws and policies built upon racism and with the
accompanying explosion in formal racial theories. During his
lifetime Roosevelt saw the transformation of Charles Darwin's
theories of evolution and natural selection into all-encompass-
ing laws of "survival of the fittest" in which social and biological theory were uncritically mixed invariably to define the "fittest" so as to exclude nonwhites and ethnics. Roosevelt also
witnessed the alteration of the less explicitly racist assumptions of the historico-literary tradition of Anglo-Saxonism into
justifications for imperialistic destinies shared by members of
the "English-speaking race." In addition, he and other American intellectuals were profoundly influenced by the emergence
of a plethora of racial theories grounded in the natural sciences
and elaborated upon by the practitioners of the emergent social sciences.

In the intellectual ambience of the late nineteenth century, it would have been remarkable if any individual with Roosevelt's interests and inclinations had not developed a fondness for the discussion of race and race theory, but TR, like every youth who grew up in an atmosphere of Victorian privilege, was bombarded from early childhood with ideas which stressed the superiority of the white race and the inferiority of non-whites. Through the formative years and into adulthood, he moved in an environment where race often dominated discussion and was nearly always present in any intellectual exchange. Although the precise origins of each element in his personal racial ideology cannot be traced, the general ways in which the dominant milieu shaped his racial cosmology are reasonably clear.

Roosevelt's family background and education were of particular importance to his emerging sense of racial consciousness. From early childhood, he studied with a succession of private tutors whom his father had chosen with characteristic care. Under the direction of these instructors he developed a fondness for literature and soon began to read omnivorously, plowing through substantial literary works at a very young age and reading for pleasure in children's periodicals. In much of his reading the precocious Theodore encountered the inevitable stereotypes of the day and in at least some of the volumes he discovered themes of white superiority. By age thirteen, he had devoured the works of James Fenimore Cooper, books which emphasized the virile racial character of the American frontiersman. He also gloried in Longfellow's *Saga of King Olaf*, which celebrated the Nordic tradition, a key ingredient in nineteenth-century theories of white supremacy.[1] In addition, while spending a summer in Dresden at age fourteen, he worked his way through the *Nibelungenlied*, a source which helped to shape an awareness of Teutonic tradition and a lifelong sense of racial kinship with the German people.[2] TR's fre-

---

1. Theodore Roosevelt, *An Autobiography* in Herman Hagedorn (ed.), *The Works of Theodore Roosevelt* (24 vols; New York, 1925), XXII, 26–27.
2. *Ibid.*, 23.

quent allusions to the German classic during the next forty years testified to the strong influence of the Teutonic myth upon his intellectual development, and in composing his own epic of the American frontier, *The Winning of the West*, he drew close parallels between Siegfried, the "hard-fighting, hard drinking, boastful hero of Nieblung [*sic*] fame," and the equally heroic American frontiersman "of a thousand years later " whose recklessness, tenacity, and bravura thrilled the young historian. Above all else, however, the mythical Siegfried and the legendary frontiersman were hunters of superhuman capacity and TR toasted their accomplishments with an extravagant excerpt from the epic:

> Danach schlug er weider einen Buffel und einen Elk
> Vier starkes Auer neider und einen grimmen Schelk,
> So schnell trug ihn die Mähre, dasz ihm nichts entsprang;
> Hinden und Hirsche wurden viele sein Fang.
> . . . . . . ein Waldthier fürchterlich,
> Einen wilden Bären.[3]

The influence of classical German and American literature upon the developing world view of the child Roosevelt was supplemented by extensive reading in popular literature and periodicals. Among the magazines that young Roosevelt read was *Our Young Folks*, a publication intended to entertain children and to instill regard for traditional morality as well. Like virtually all of the popular press of the period, *Our Young Folks* conveyed a host of racial stereotypes and mythology and TR,

---

3. Thereafter he knocked down again a buffalo and an elk
   Four strong mighty oxen and a furious schelk,
   His mare bore him so swiftly that nothing escaped him;
   Many hart and hind became his prey
   . . . . . . a terrible animal is the forest,
   a wild bear.
   Roosevelt commented in his footnote that "Siegfried's elk was our moose; and, like the American frontiersman of to-day, the old German singer calls the Wisent or bison a buffalo—European sportsmen now committing an equally bad blunder by giving it the name of the extinct aurochs. Be it observed also that the hard-fighting, hard-drinking, boastful hero of Nieblung [*sic*] fame used a 'spür hund' just as his representative of Kentucky or Tennessee used a track-hound a thousand years later." TR, *The Winning of the West*, in *Works*, X, 132n.

like most children who read the magazine, accepted the racial notions that appeared in its pages. In Roosevelt's case the influence seems to have been particularly strong, powerful enough at least to prompt him to recall years later the similarity between the servants who populated the magazine stories and those who resided in the Roosevelt household. For the mature TR, his four black servants were "really the best representatives of the devoted colored family servant type, their attitude varying from one of warm, personal friendship to the injured dignity of a big child detected in shortcomings." The "native American" servants of the household, TR wrote his sister, "might have walked out of the pages of *Our Young Folks*."[4]

While young Roosevelt had early imbibed these notions, he had also developed a critical sensitivity to several areas of formal learning and acquired a special passion for natural science by the time he was seven years old. His lifelong affection for science and his firm belief that nature's creatures could be classified had roots in the careful cataloging of the habits and appearances of the varieties of small animals and birds he met on numerous forays through the Long Island woods and on tramps in the wild. Longer journeys such as the excursion with his father to the Middle East in 1872 gave him unusual opportunities for observation. On this trip the fourteen-year-old Roosevelt committed to his diary scores of sketches and hundreds of details on wildlife but also included his reaction to a first encounter with an array of humans who, like other animals, appeared to belong to sharply differentiated types. Theodore related in his diary how he had marveled at "various races of men" in a Cairo procession, races like "the white, black, Egyptian and Eastern whites, Arab or Syrian." It had been, he noted, the most interesting hour of his life.[5]

Not all of young Roosevelt's encounters with race were so scientific. A childish cruelty in frightening black maids at the

4. TR to Anna Roosevelt Cowles, July 28, 1911, in Elting E. Morison (ed.), *The Letters of Theodore Roosevelt* (8 vols.; Cambridge, Mass., 1951) VII, 316. Hereinafter cited as *Letters*.
5. TR, *Theodore Roosevelt's Diaries of His Boyhood and Youth* (New York, 1928), 289.

family's New Jersey retreat may have been "natural" behavior
for many northern children reared in late-nineteenth-century
America, but Theodore also had the stimulus of a southern-
born mother with a heritage that stressed membership in a superior race.[6] As he recalled years later in his autobiography, her
wistful recollections of antebellum southern life and the folk
tales of black life which she related impressed him greatly.[7]
Such commonly held views of racial superiority needed little
reinforcement in the racially obsessive late nineteenth century,
but to a bright, sensitive child like Theodore, who read widely
and listened carefully, the idea of race must have seemed especially important.

For the remainder of his pre-college years a life of both racial privilege and inherited wealth kept him largely free from
contact with nonwhites, and when he arrived at Harvard College in the fall of 1876 after two years of intensive tutoring,
contact with nonwhites remained infrequent. However, young
Roosevelt soon encountered an intellectual atmosphere perva-
sive with racially oriented topics and a campus dominated by
intellectuals who subscribed to racially deterministic philosophies. While the times dictated that racial motifs would concern nearly all the faculty and permeate many disciplines, even
the well-prepared and favorably predisposed young Roosevelt
may not have anticipated the emphasis given to race in the
college.

Many of the subjects which he took at Harvard offered specific opportunities for discussion of racial themes and especially for examination of the ideas of Teutonic superiority familiar since childhood. Teutonic germ theory, Darwinism, and
a romantic Anglo-Saxonism dominated much of the tone of the
college, and Roosevelt's course of study brought close contact
with substantial elements of each. "German Historical Prose,"
taken in the sophomore year, likely reinforced beliefs about the
racial superiority of Teutons as did an advanced course, "Rich-

6. Carleton Putnam, *Theodore Roosevelt: The Formative Years* (New York, 1958),
31.
7. TR, *An Autobiography*, in *Works*, XXII, 3–9.

ter, Goethe, and German Lyrics" the following year. These courses no doubt strengthened Roosevelt's already powerful regard for the German literary tradition and provided a basis for his belief that linguistic and racial superiority were closely related. During the Harvard years and for nearly a decade thereafter, these ideas governed his thinking about race and parallel subjects.[8]

During the last two years in Cambridge he gradually turned away from his youthful resolve to become a naturalist, toward plans for a life in politics and government. At that time TR came under the influence of Harvard professor Nathaniel Southgate Shaler, a geologist, historian, and naturalist who enthusiastically accepted notions of white supremacy, innate black immorality, and the desirability of slavery as an instrument of necessary racial "adjustment." Shaler's personal background, as well as his intellectual interests, bore sharp similarities to Roosevelt's. He was a dedicated Unionist with deep ties to the South, whose mother, like TR's, had come from a prominent southern family with strong attachments to the slave system. As a student at Harvard in the late 1850s, he developed interests in paleontology and zoology and became a disciple of Jean Lamarck, the French naturalist who argued for the survival of species through physical adaptation to the environment. Shaler's interests, like Roosevelt's, extended beyond science into history and he wrote a chronicle of the Kentucky frontier and several other works of historical scholarship which contained a number of themes attractive to TR. In these books and in his scientific treatises, he emphasized the importance of "character" in "social evolution," posited the development of an American "race," and stressed that the best representative of the American "type" could be found in his native Kentucky and in New England. Shaler's belief in the racial superiority of the white American led him to fear that the immigration of

8. For discussions of Roosevelt's student days, see Donald Wilhelm, *Theodore Roosevelt as an Undergraduate* (Boston, 1910); J. Lawrence Laughlin, "Roosevelt at Harvard," *Review of Reviews*, LXX (1924), 512–14; Curtis Guild, Jr., "TR at Harvard," *Harvard Graduate Magazine*, X (1938), 177–83.

"alien races" could eventually induce a watering down of the old stock which would diminish the quality of the "American race." Blacks, in Shaler's view, were of thoroughly inferior racial stock, largely insusceptible to formal education, and possessed of too much political power for their own well-being. According to Shaler, the ultimate admission of the black into membership in American society depended solely upon acceptance of white domination.[9]

Strikingly similar points of view appeared in Roosevelt's early scholarly efforts, published soon after leaving Harvard. TR also believed that the environment could alter racial types; like Shaler he believed that a distinctively American race existed and considered the Kentuckian the best representative of that type. Not only did he share Shaler's Lamarckianism but he also agreed that Americans were quicker witted and more adaptable to change than the other white "races." Probably the greatest difference between the points of view of the two men lay in Roosevelt's less overtly hostile attitude toward blacks and his rejection of the justifiability of lynching, a method of social control which his mentor did not condemn outright. In later life, Roosevelt directly acknowledged the powerful influence that Shaler had exercised upon him, but even without such direct attribution, the similarity of ideas between teacher and student amply demonstrates the kinship of their points of view.

After Harvard, Roosevelt studied for a year at Columbia University, where racial theories were also held in high esteem. Although he had come to Columbia for legal studies, he found time to work with one of America's most committed "Teutonist" exponents of white superiority, John Burgess, professor of political science and author of *Political Science and Comparative Constitutional Law*, a book stressing racial impacts on governmental forms. In Burgess, Roosevelt found a racial de-

9. Thomas F. Gossett, *Race: The History of an Idea in America* (New York, 1965), 281; Nathaniel S. Shaler, *The Autobiography of Nathaniel Southgate Shaler* (New York, 1909); Idus A. Newby, *Jim Crow's Defense: Anti-Negro Thought in America, 1900–1930* (Baton Rouge, 1965), 133, 147.

terminist who particularly valued the idea that the "Teutonic Races" must recognize their unique talent for political organization. Like Shaler, Burgess also held low opinions of non-whites and called for the Teuton to fulfill his responsibility to eliminate "barbaric populations" which resisted "civilized man." The Columbia professor denounced the excess of "weak sentimentality abroad in the world" that originated in the "lack of discrimination in regard to the capacities of races." Arguments like Burgess' which deplored sentimentality while emphasizing strength were persuasive to Roosevelt, and the profound influence of Burgess' racial theories can be detected in the histories that Roosevelt wrote before 1889.[10]

Bored by law school, the twenty-three-year-old Roosevelt left in 1881 to run for a seat in the New York Assembly. By that time he had been thoroughly exposed to two of the most influential race theorists of the day and had also heard the arguments of prominent social Darwinists like William Graham Sumner, the Yale economist, and Francis A. Walker, M.I.T. political economist and pioneer demographer, both of whom addressed a club at Harvard that young TR had helped to organize. Through his voracious reading, Roosevelt had also explored the writings of historian Francis Parkman, whose harsh estimates of the American Indian influenced TR's developing appreciation for the importance of race on the frontier.

In 1884, after the death of his mother and his wife, Roosevelt retreated to his North Dakota ranch and, between episodes of hunting trips, roundups, and outlaw chasing, poured out a series of books interlarded with passages extolling the racial superiority of the white American, deploring the decadence of the Indian, and celebrating the power of the American environment to assimilate and homogenize diverse racial groups. Roosevelt had learned well the lessons of Anglo-Saxonism, Lamarckianism, and Teutonism studied at Harvard and Columbia, and virtually all of these books disclosed the powerful im-

10. Gossett, *Race*, 113; See Chapter III herein.

pact of such theories on his mind. Even a book like *Hunting Trips of a Ranchman*, written primarily for a popular audience, was rife with racial themes, while more scholarly works including *The Winning of the West* depended, like his first work of historical scholarship, *The Naval War of 1812*, upon acceptance of the ideology of white racial destiny and supremacy. In biographies of Gouverneur Morris and Thomas Hart Benton, Roosevelt not only confirmed his beliefs in such palpable racial themes as Anglo-Saxonism, Teutonism, and social Darwinism but also revealed the late-nineteenth-century race theorist's fascination with genealogy as he delved deeply into the family histories of both men to draw conclusions about the character and ability of each based upon ethnic heritage. In all of his early writings, the young author linked racial matters with the exuberant nationalism which would come to be a Rooseveltian trademark.[11]

During the next phase of his life as he moved toward involvement in national affairs, Roosevelt's dedication to a hubristic Americanism became even more closely tied to racial theory. In the period between his assumption of a position as United States Civil Service commissioner in 1889 until his elevation to the presidency in 1901, TR's orientation in racial theory would shift away from romantic Anglo-Saxonism and Teutonism, toward involvement in racial theories with a social-scientific flavor. TR's racial thought would continue to bear the lasting impress of Shaler, Burgess, Parkman, and other professors and fellow students of the Harvard and Columbia years, but he gradually broadened his circle of intellectual acquaintances and developed a continuing dialogue with prominent thinkers of backgrounds and interests similar to his.

The six years in Washington from 1889 until 1895 provided Roosevelt the opportunity to expand his intellectual horizons and to consider a potpourri of new ideas about race and policy matters that had racial dimensions. Increasingly, the topic of

11. See Chapter III herein.

American expansionism came to occupy much of his concern and it was with an old friend, Henry Cabot Lodge, that Roosevelt conversed and corresponded most about an American policy of imperialistic expansion. With Lodge and with Captain Alfred Mahan, the theorist of naval power and imperialism, TR probed the implications of such a departure. The three agreed that Americans, as members of a superior race, had not only an obligation but a sacred duty to extend their sway over lesser peoples and to guide and tutor the inhabitants of the benighted areas of the world in the lessons of American democracy. A student of power politics as well as racial theory, Roosevelt knew that in the last analysis, the enormous economic and strategic advantages of the United States would decide the success of any American imperialistic ventures, but he together with Lodge, Mahan, and scores of others who dreamed of an American empire justified such a policy on racial grounds.

Lodge's racial ideas, like Roosevelt's, had been formed in an atmosphere of privilege and wealth. A graduate student at Harvard during the period when TR was an undergraduate, he had been one of the students in Henry Adams' famous seminar on the Anglo-Saxon origins of American political institutions. After Adams left Harvard, Lodge carried on the work which admittedly sought links between Teutonic racial superiority and American political forms. Now, as a young member of the House of Representatives, he propounded his racial theories on the floor of the United States Congress and in one widely reported speech revealed the importance he attached to race and the gigantic influence which he believed that it exercised in human affairs. For Lodge, individual races possessed

> moral and intellectual characters, which in their association make the soul of a race, and which represent the product of all its past, the inheritance of all its ancestors, and the motives of its conduct. The men of each race possess an indestructible stock of ideas, traditions, sentiments, modes of thoughts, an unconscious inheritance from their ancestors, upon which argument had no effect. What makes a race are their mental, and above all, their moral characteristics, the slow growth and assimilation of centuries of

toil and conflict. These are the qualities . . . which make one race rise and another fall.[12]

Roosevelt wrote his friend to say that he thought the speech "A-1," and Lodge wrote back to say that he had been substantially influenced by the writings of the French theorist Gustave LeBon. Indeed, much of what Lodge had said in the Congress had been borrowed directly from the Frenchman who argued that individual races had "souls," that true races rarely existed in a state of purity, and that "historical" races were in a constant process of formation. Like many other race theorists, LeBon emphasized a hierarchy of races and stressed that individual races developed specific psychologies or characters. At Lodge's insistence, Roosevelt quickly read LeBon's theories and, while he dissented from some of the Frenchman's findings, he pronounced the racial arguments to be "very fine and true."[13]

TR's racial education during the Washington years often followed this familiar pattern. A friend or acquaintance would suggest particularly cogent works which Roosevelt would read and incorporate into his own theories. On occasion, when the future president felt strongly about a particular book, he would seek out opportunities to review it for a scholarly or popular journal. Such reviews allowed Roosevelt to air his views on race and to gain the attention of the reading public. Such was the case with his review of Charles Pearson's *National Life and Character*. The Australian author's book was the rage in the intellectual circles in which Roosevelt moved during 1894 and 1895 and TR wrote an extremely long review for the *Sewanee Review*. While he rejected some of Pearson's racial observations, including the assertions that third-world people would eventually pose a military threat to the "dominant" races, he warmly endorsed other arguments, in particular the notion that the "dominant" races must guard carefully against a decline in "character" among their group and the associated idea

12. Quoted in Gary B. Nash and Richard Weiss (eds.), *The Great Fear: Race in the Mind of America* (New York, 1970), 134.
13. TR to Henry Cabot Lodge, April 29, 1896, in *Letters*, I, 535, 535n.

that they should pay special heed to the erosion of the family unit.[14]

Roosevelt began to develop an interest in the latter concept during his Washington days, and concern that the dominant races were not reproducing in sufficient numbers to guarantee their survival ultimately became TR's greatest fear. Another close friend, Cecil Arthur Spring-Rice, an English diplomat and scholar, added significantly to Roosevelt's racial education in this area. Spring-Rice and Roosevelt met during the late 1880s and began a correspondence which continued for the remainder of TR's life. Like Lodge and Mahan, the Englishman was an ardent imperialist who shared his generation's vision for a world dominated by the English-speaking peoples. The threat that these "dominant people" might not be producing enough of their own kind to ensure their ultimate triumph troubled Spring-Rice nearly as much as it did Roosevelt, and their letters often turned toward the subject as they considered other matters of racial and international importance.

During the same years, Roosevelt developed a correspondence with a number of prominent intellectuals of the day including the poet laureate of the international imperialist movement, Rudyard Kipling, and the British historian Sir George Otto Trevelyan, whom Roosevelt found an especially willing auditor for his theories on the future of the "English-speaking race." Toward the end of this phase of Roosevelt's racial education the civil servant became a military man and left for Cuba to pick up the white man's burden. In passage, Roosevelt read Edmond Demolin's *Supériorité des Anglo-Saxons*, surely a fitting preparation for battle against the "decadent" Spaniards.[15] Roosevelt's two-year term as governor of New York and his six-month tenure as vice-president found him primarily occupied with politics and matters of state, but soon after his succession to the presidency, his interest in race reappeared stronger than ever. Perhaps because he now faced a multitude of policy questions with racial overtones, TR increased his correspondence

14. TR, "National Life and Character," in *Works*, XIV, 230–57.
15. TR, *The Rough Riders*, in *Works*, XIII, 36.

with prominent race thinkers and social theorists concerned with race.

Although President Roosevelt favored discussion of racial matters with broad policy implications, he found time to continue his prodigious reading pace and absorbed numerous scholarly works that dealt with racial theory. For example, many of his developing ideas on race decadence came from the English scholar-statesman Arthur James Balfour, whose book *Decadence* he read in 1908.[16] Roosevelt also explored numerous other European works with Darwinian themes, including Hans Dreisch's *The Science and Philosophy of the Organism* as well as the works of Anton Dohrn and Sir William Ridgeway, books which posed questions about the relative importance of environment and heredity in racial theory.[17] In addition, Roosevelt reported that he had read with difficulty (in the original Italian) the work of E. de Michelis, *L'Origine degli Indo-Europei*, as well as the works of Giuseppe Sergi on the Mediterranean "races."[18]

The gamut of Roosevelt's racial reading and thus his racial education ranged broadly during the presidential years. Although he would have rejected the idea that the more vulgar race theorists like Charles Carroll (author of *The Negro a Beast*) had anything to add to his racial education, he thoroughly explored the writings of adamant racial determinists like Madison Grant and Houston Stewart Chamberlain whose major works belonged to the same intellectual genre as the racial theories of the German Fascists of the 1920s and 1930s. At the other extreme, Roosevelt read and commented upon at least one "radical" theorist of race, the French social theorist Jean Finot. Finot approached problems of race in a most unusual fashion with the arguments that the concept of race really had little mean-

16. TR to Arthur James Balfour, March 5, 1908, in *Letters*, VI, 959.
17. TR to James J. Walsh, February 23, 1909, *ibid.*, VI, 1535; TR to Henry Fairfield Osborn, December 21, 1908, *ibid.*, VI, 1435.
18. TR to Benjamin Ide Wheeler, May 11, 1904, *ibid.*, IV, 795; TR to Herbert Putnam, October 18, 1902, *ibid.*, III, 344; E. de Michelis, *L'Origine degli Indo-Europei* (Turin, 1903); Guiseppe Sergi, *The Mediterranean Race: A Study of the Origin of European Peoples* (New York, 1901).

ing, that racial terminology often proved empty and vague, and
that much of race theory was little better than myth. Roosevelt
thought Finot's principal book, *Race Prejudice*, contained important material and recommended it to several of his acquaintances including Albert Shaw, the prominent race thinker and
editor of the *Review of Reviews*.[19]

During the presidency, Roosevelt relied most heavily, however, on the thought of American theorists—social scientists,
scientists, and historians who shared his belief that civilization,
history, and the natural world could be profitably understood
in a racial paradigm. At various times TR consulted such prominent intellectuals as Charles Benedict Davenport, director of
the Eugenics Records Office, David Starr Jordan, ichthyologist,
eugenicist, and president of Stanford University, and Benjamin
Ide Wheeler, president of the University of California. In addition, he drew ideas on racial matters from historians like James
Ford Rhodes, who influenced TR's understanding of the role
of blacks in American history. Gradually, however, Roosevelt
came to rely principally on two scholars for intellectual guid-
ance in the racial area: Edward Alsworth Ross, a Lamarckian
sociologist who taught at the University of Wisconsin, and
Henry Fairfield Osborn, director of New York's Museum of
Natural History, prominent paleontologist, and author of *The
Origin and Evolution of Life*.

Ross advanced Roosevelt's racial education in several important areas. For advice and information about the "Chinese
question," for example, TR looked to the Wisconsin sociologist, who advocated severe restrictions on Oriental immigration with the argument that social upheaval would inevitably
result from the clash between Orientals and white Americans
on the Pacific slope. At one point Roosevelt wrote to tell Ross
that he had opened a speech on Chinese exclusion with a quo-
tation from one of his books. "Of course I am with you absolutely about Chinese exclusion and Asiatic exclusion gener-

19. TR to Albert Shaw, April 3, 1907, in *Letters*, V, 637.

ally," Roosevelt wrote, and went on to observe that it astonished him that "so many of our reformers[,] men like Ray Stannard Baker for instance, are utterly ignorant of the fact that far seeing men wish us now to have fortification and navies primarily to protect our democracy if it is ever menaced by some great Asiatic military power."[20]

Ross had coined the term *race suicide* and he often stressed the grave importance of designing federal policies to deal with the "threat" to American racial integrity posed by that phenomenon. In addition, Roosevelt's strong endorsement of Ross's best-known book, *Social Control*, suggested that he and the sociologist had similar understandings about the relationship between race and social reform. When Roosevelt wrote to Ross to comment on the desirability of "standardizing" old-stock American families at four to six children, he suggested that powerful corporations intended to thwart the reformist tendencies of his administration by circulating reports ridiculing the president's belief in race suicide, with the allegations that TR advocated twelve to fifteen children for all American families. In this instance and in others, Ross reassured Roosevelt of the essential correctness of their jointly held beliefs and reinforced the close alliance between racial theories and public policy in the president's mind.[21]

On occasion, Roosevelt attempted to educate Ross in racial matters. After reading Alexander Sutherland's *The Origin and Growth of the Moral Instinct*, a two-volume tome heavy with racial emphases, the president recommended it to his scholarly friend, but in typical Rooseveltian fashion quibbled with some of Sutherland's observations about the racial characteristics of European types. "My memory," Roosevelt told the sociologist, "is that the European southern brunettes are not square-headed, but long-headed. The medium-tinted middle

20. TR to Edward A. Ross, October 31, 1911, in Theodore Roosevelt Collection, Library of Congress.

21. TR to Edward A. Ross, November 2, 1904 and June 15, 1908, in Roosevelt Collection, Library of Congress.

Europeans are square-headed; the northern blondes are again long-headed." [22]

Like many other race theorists, Roosevelt thought that race had implications and importance far beyond mere social and political concerns and in fact believed that racial theory and associated ideas could be useful in explaining all of history as well as contemporary human behavior. Thus, in 1908 when the president accepted an invitation to deliver the Romanes Lecture at Oxford University, he chose as his topic "Biological Analogies in History" and composed a sweeping examination of the whole of human history which stressed the intimate relationships between evolution, race, and the development of civilization. For the special advice and assistance needed in preparation of the lecture, Roosevelt turned to another intellectual ally, Henry Fairfield Osborn.

The two men had been friends since the late 1890s, but in the last years of the Roosevelt presidency Osborn emerged as one of Roosevelt's closest intellectual advisors. More extreme in his racial views than TR, Osborn used his intimate knowledge of paleontology to promote the idea that some races were older than others and as a result that "primitive races" and blacks in particular were retarded both physically and mentally. He ultimately accepted the extreme notion that races represented separate species of men, an idea often advanced by early-twentieth-century racists to justify repressive social and political policies. [23]

Roosevelt's racial education continued throughout the last years of his life, but the vigor which had characterized the racial discussions of earlier times now faded as TR's circle of race theorists simultaneously narrowed. From 1913 until his death in 1919, letters from old friends like Lodge, Spring-Rice, Ross, and Osborn disclosed fewer racial themes than before. While TR maintained an interest in a number of different areas of

22. TR to Edward A. Ross, June 15, 1908, in Roosevelt Collection, Library of Congress.

23. Newby, *Jim Crow's Defense*, 22–23. For TR's relationship with Osborn and the influence of the latter on the writing of "Biological Analogies in History," see Chapter II herein.

racial thought he became more and more obsessed with the spectre of race suicide and confined much of his thought to this topic and published numerous articles written to educate wider popular audiences on the racial and national penalties of insufficient procreation.

Roosevelt did attempt to keep up with newer developments in related theories during the last five years of his life, but much of what he said and wrote about race marked his ideas as products of an earlier age. Although he had divested himself of the clichés of Aryanism, Anglo-Saxonism, and Teutonism, a strong commitment to neo-Lamarckianism remained despite the precipitous decline in the popularity of that theory toward the end of the second decade of this century. Similarly, Roosevelt's comments upon some aspects of racial theory reflected a stronger concern with cranial characteristics of "races" than that of most of his fellow neo-Lamarckians. In exchanges with Madison Grant, author of the thoroughly racist diatribe *The Passing of the Great Race*, Roosevelt insisted on relating cranial typology to cultural behavior. Even Grant, who purveyed one of the harshest of the racially deterministic philosophies, did not adhere to Roosevelt's slightly shopworn theories of skull type and race; nor did he subscribe to the similarly outmoded notion of a plural concept of race which TR resolutely retained. (See page 28.) Grant corrected the former president in his usage of the term *race* itself when Roosevelt referred to skull size of Jewish people as a determinant of racial characteristics. "As for the long and short headed Jews," Grant told TR, "I think we have here a *people* and not a *race*, that is a group of diverse origins with very marked and persistent secondary characteristics imposed on them through prolonged isolation." [24]

The relationship with Grant brought to a close a lifelong education in matters of race and TR's endorsement of *The Passing of the Great Race* illustrated the limits of his receptivity to new ideas, as does his apparent lack of knowledge of the revolutionary investigations into race of younger anthropologists like

24. Madison Grant to TR, December 2, 1916 and May 27, 1918, in Roosevelt Collection, Library of Congress.

Roland B. Dixon and Franz Boas. In the final analysis Roosevelt's racial education was a part of his larger education and his circle of racial speculators part of a more extensive intellectual world. Aside from his political power, the factor which gave particular force to his observations on race can be traced to his substantial standing among many scholars and writers. From the sheer volume of Roosevelt's writings one could conclude that he was at the very least prolific, his published works running to twenty-four large volumes on history, anthropology, science, and other areas of concern to intellectuals. He wrote a multi-volume history, several biographies and single-volume histories, numerous scientific treatises, essay reviews, and several books which recounted his travels and observations of the world's cultures and people, all of which helped to gain a respectful hearing for his racial theories.[25]

In his own time Roosevelt earned the approbation of scholarly men for his intellectual accomplishments. The eminent historian Frederick Jackson Turner praised young Roosevelt for his literary ability and his research techniques. James Brander Mathews, professor of comparative literature at Columbia and a friend of Roosevelt's, asserted that TR had distinguished himself as a "man of letters." Roosevelt, said Mathews, "had the gift of the winged phrase, keenly pointed and barbed to flesh itself in the memory."[26] Prominent figures in the field of natural science regarded Roosevelt as an able amateur zoologist

25. Roosevelt read as prodigiously as he wrote. When Nicholas Murray Butler asked him what sort of books he had been reading, Roosevelt listed fifty or sixty read during a two-year period while president. Among the volumes were numerous histories including Macaulay's *Essays*, "three or four volumes of Gibbon," Carlyle's *Frederick the Great*, Hay and Nicolay's *Lincoln* and two volumes of Lincoln's *Speeches and Writing*. The latter, Roosevelt commented, he had "not only read through," but had read "parts again and again." In addition, he had devoured works by Francis Bacon, Shakespeare, Drayton, Hugo, and a host of lesser lights. Among the popular works which he read were five novels by Owen Wister: *The Virginian, Red Men and White, Philosophy Four, Lady Baltimore,* and *Lin McClean*, all with themes which celebrated the Anglo-Saxon "type." TR to Nicholas Murray Butler, November 4, 1903, in *Letters*, III, 641–44.

26. See Turner's reviews of Roosevelt's *The Winning of the West*, in *The Dial*, X (1889), 71–73; *The Nation*, LX (1895), 240–42; *The Nation*, LXIII (1892), 277; *American Historical Review*, II (1896), 171–76. For Mathews' comment see *Works*, XIV, xi.

and his lifelong correspondence with Osborn provides a record of interesting exchanges on a variety of scientific topics. Moreover, Roosevelt's reviews of scientific works, his study of protective coloration among small animals, his contributions to the debate on the nature of species and the war against the "nature fakers" during his presidential administration testified to considerable expertise.[27]

In addition to the high opinions of his fellow American intellectuals, perhaps the greatest acknowledgment of Roosevelt's scholarly abilities came from the faculties of three of the world's great universities. In 1910, emerging from the African bush after a year's tramping, Roosevelt delivered lectures at the Sorbonne, the University of Berlin, and Oxford. The invitation to deliver the Romanes Lecture at Oxford, reserved for the world's distinguished natural scientists, pleased Roosevelt immensely and he exerted special efforts in the last months of his presidency in the preparation of the lengthy essay, his most important statement on race. One Oxford don commented after the presentation that the faculty inclined to give the lecturer an "Alpha Plus" and the lecture a "Beta Minus," a reflection it seems of Roosevelt's personal popularity and the high academic standards at the English institution.[28]

Although Roosevelt gained his expertise from the world's most eminent race theorists, it might be argued that because of his enormous popularity TR became the most effective racial educator of all. In his multiple careers as journalist, historian, scientist, and politician Roosevelt said and wrote much about racial theory and racial beliefs that helped to set the tone for the American understanding of the concept. As a prolific author and popularizer of racial thought, he wielded enormous influence on the development of the American understanding of race and he contributed significantly to the scholarly discussion of the topic as well. If he did not rival William James and John Dewey as creative thinkers, he did function as a serious

27. For a favorable assessment of Roosevelt as a scientist see Paul Russell Cutright, *Theodore Roosevelt the Naturalist* (New York, 1956).
28. Henry F. Pringle, *Theodore Roosevelt: A Biography* (New York, 1931), 520.

intellectual and as an influential popularizer whose racial theories deserve careful analysis. Thus, TR's education began in childhood, developed in the environment of the dominant racial ideologies at Harvard and Columbia, and matured in a context of solemn intellectual exchange with the world's most eminent race thinkers. It was a very thorough education.

CHAPTER II

Theory

Theodore Roosevelt's lifetime coincided with the zenith of racist thought in America. From his birth in 1858 until his death in 1919, the twenty-sixth president of the United States developed a formal approach to race based upon the best contemporary scholarly opinion. His racial ideology seen within the context of early twentieth-century scholarship is perhaps most remarkable for its orthodox congruency with the more advanced speculation of the day, whether in anthropology or in areas of natural science which impinged upon racial theory.

Roosevelt, broadly acquainted with scientific and social scientific theories and possessing a penchant for intellectual orderliness, saw the concept of race as a cogent way to bring order, regularity, and consistency to human differences. To explain history, society, and individual and group character in racial terms appeared both logical and scientific in the light of the best scholarly opinion of the day. Moreover, there seemed to be little reason to doubt the validity of the concept itself; "race" had been legitimized by a century or more of scholarship and scientific investigation and, in the supercharged atmosphere of theorizing at the turn of the century, the integrity of the race concept was rarely questioned. That "races" existed seemed indisputable. More debatable were specific issues relating to the precise meaning and relative importance of the race idea, and these provided the focus for much of the intellectual conversation on race during that time.

Like most Americans, Roosevelt made an a priori assumption that races existed. His conceptualization of race and his racial theories can be best understood by analyzing the idiom in which he discussed race and by an appraisal of the character of his formal ideas about race. Roosevelt himself recognized the terminological difficulties in discussing racial theory. Dissatisfied with both the imprecision and the inadequacy of the language for this purpose, he confided to Thomas St. John Gaffney, in 1905, that "all of our terminology in race questions is usually employed incorrectly."[1] Nevertheless, he had been and remained a prisoner of turn-of-the-century racial language, formal terminology, and jargon which locked his and many other minds into a racial Weltanschauung.

The language of Roosevelt and his fellow theorists now has a decidedly anachronistic flavor. To some extent technical jargon, the words and phrases used by those who thought about racial theory constitute a conceptual edifice distinctly different from the framework in which racial theory is discussed today. Many of the terms, phrases, and words employed in late nineteenth century race thinking have passed out of usage; others have specifically altered meanings and still others have contextual connotations unfamiliar even to the specialist. To understand Roosevelt's racial thought requires an awareness of the special language he used to discuss race.

In approaching the study of a body of popular assumptions, concepts, superstitions, and beliefs, historians would do well to note the admonitions of the pioneer linguist Edward Sapir, who early recognized the dynamic qualities of language. Sapir, introducing the concept of linguistic drift, argued that "language moves down time in a current of its own making. It has a *drift*. ... Nothing is perfectly static. Every word, every sound and accent is a slowly changing configuration, moulded by the invisible and impersonal *drift* that is the life of language."[2]

Historians must not only consider the dynamic qualities of language but also must explore thoroughly the relationships between nonlinguistic and linguistic events—the interplay between culture and language. By careful analysis of the lan-

1. TR to Thomas St. John Gaffney, May 10, 1901, in *Letters*, III, 76.
2. Quoted in Stephen Ullmann, *Semantics, the Science of Meaning* (London 1967), 193.

guage of the subject or subject-idea under investigation, the scholar may not only "explain" more accurately but may more effectively and precisely convey something of the flavor of an age or of an idea. Particularly in racial topics is there an urge to superimpose contemporary definitions on past language, a tendency to ignore the "slowly changing configuration" that is the idiom for racial theory.

Between 1875 and 1905, a period when racial theories became increasingly more complicated and inclusive, the English language, descriptively inadequate for the racial occurrences of the late nineteenth century, underwent rather abrupt and startling changes. These changes, for the most part additions to the social terminology of race thinking, quickly became indispensable to the discussions of practically all areas of racial thought. Around 1875, for example, *race consciousness* came into usage. Soon, other terms, descriptive of but by no means limited to relations between blacks and whites, attained widespread usage and became familiar concepts to race theorists. *Race conflict, race feeling, race issue, race line, race prejudice, race problem, race question, race riot*, and *race war* all found niches in the spoken and written language during Roosevelt's lifetime.[3]

Each of these terms describes a condition or state which relates to the self-awareness of white racial superiority or the sense of separation and conflict which had become part and parcel of American race relations. *Race feeling* and *race consciousness* in particular suggest the quasi-mystical qualities associated with racial identity. The other terms also connote a self-knowledge of race membership which approximates the concept of fellow feeling, originated by Charles Horton Cooley in 1909. Each also implicitly suggests that these traits belonged largely to groups capable of recognizing them and to those possessing an awareness of the importance of racial identity.

Terms like *race conflict, race issue, race line, race problem, race question, race riot*, and *race war* reveal a growing conflict

3. Mitford M. Mathews, *A Dictionary of Americanisms on Historical Principles* (Chicago, 1951), 465.

orientation within the language of race. Each term indicates, in something of a progression, an increasing acceptance of the inevitability of racial conflict. The sudden appearance of each of these terms in the language during a very brief span of time, linguistically, suggests how quickly language modified and adjusted to an intensification of the race theme.

Although Theodore Roosevelt's racial lexicon contained most of the newer catchwords and phrases and some more traditional technical terms, it also had an idiosyncratic flavor. Conscious of the power and importance of language, he often stressed the necessity for precision when discussing any serious matter. One of his most famous intellectual encounters, the celebrated debate with Hart Merriam over the nature of species, rested almost exclusively on questions of definition and semantics.

Roosevelt took particular care to define terms crucial to his racial world view. For example, the concept of "blood," a word used with great frequency by race theorists, carried strong connotations of the inheritability of specific character traits. The "success" of the American frontier experience, Roosevelt explained, could be largely understood in terms of blood. In an early discussion on the traits of members of the old families of the Atlantic seaboard who had gone to the frontier, he explained that "blood" largely accounted for their quick assumption of leadership roles, and in a passage which probed both the meaning of the word and its importance for racial theory, Roosevelt showed his strong penchant for precision in the language of race theory: "They [the aristocratic frontiersmen] were of good blood—using the words as they should be used, as meaning blood that has flowed through the veins of generations of self-restraint and courage and hard work, and careful thinking in mind and in the manly virtues." Like many contemporary thinkers, Roosevelt believed that such behavioral traits were inheritable. Good blood, the source of desirable traits, was of immense importance. The frontiersmen's "inheritance of sturdy and self-reliant manhood helped them greatly," he wrote. "Their blood told in their favor as blood generally does tell when other things are equal." Here Roosevelt disclosed his general belief

that some blood types outclassed others, and that good breeding accounted for great behavioral differences among men. That
blood was a property of race he made abundantly clear. The
frontiersman, he observed, "felt that pride of race which spurs
a man to effort, instead of making him feel that he is excused
from effort. They realized that the qualities they inherited from
their forefathers ought to be further developed by them as their
forefathers had originally developed them. They knew that
their blood and breeding, though making it probable that they
would with proper effort succeed, yet entitled them to no success which they could not fairly earn in open contest with their
rivals."[4]

Roosevelt denied, however, that blood was an *all*-controlling
factor. That "blood would tell" seemed clear enough; that it
was not enough to ensure success in the frontier struggle was
equally obvious to the young historian. In this sense, although
greatly influenced by racial ideas, he did not embrace a thor-
oughgoing racial determinism allowing for no environmental
or cultural influence upon behavior.

In addition to *blood*, Roosevelt relied on a number of other
terms which were of rather common usage in racial theory, and
each indicates the presence in his mind of individual concepts
related to the idea of race. *Stock*, a fixed configuration of various race "strains," generally referred to the raw materials of
ethnicity out of which races were made. Roosevelt used *strain*
in a manner approximating the biological usage of the term,
that is to refer to a group of organisms of the same species which
have distinctive characteristics but are not a separate breed or
variety.

Besides *stock, blood,* and *strain*, Roosevelt relied frequently
on an entire set of concepts which indicated the functional
properties of race. Normally he paired the word *race* itself
with another noun or with a modifier. The two words combined
usually suggested that a human group possessed a particular
quality or function. For example, he employed various terms

4. TR, *The Winning of the West*, in *Works*, XI, 421.

expressive of racial destiny. *Race expansion* denoted the spread or extension of a particular group outside its traditional boundaries, while *subject-races* included groups who were victims of "race expansion." To understand "race expansion" and the contemporary scene one needed to understand "race-history," which meant the half-mythical record of a host of racial, ethnic, national, and local groups. *Race characteristics* described the inheritable traits possessed by such groups, while *race traditions* represented the sum of race history and inherited "race characteristics." Roosevelt also spoke of the "soul" of a race, a term which alluded to the mystical cultural heritage shared by a people. Social and historical questions of great importance had to be considered from the "race-standpoint" and in terms of "race supremacy." The "higher races," Roosevelt believed, shared a great and glorious "race-destiny." The variety and extent of Roosevelt's language of race is considerable. In fact, he was inclined, like most anthropologists of the period, to discuss practically any behavioral or cultural trait as a racial trait. *Race intermixture, race traditions, masterful race, race origin, race elements, race limits, race prejudice,* and *race-life* are just a few other key expressions which suggest the conceptual configuration in which Roosevelt's constructs of race thinking were shaped.[5]

Besides these terms and phrases, more technical terms, by their presence or absence, are important to an understanding of the form in which Roosevelt explained race. Although many Victorian theorists spoke passionately of an "Anglo-Saxon race" or an "Aryan race," Roosevelt eventually discarded them as terms inappropriate to any serious discussion of racial theory.[6] The self-consciousness with which he rejected both terms underscored the care he gave to language. "'Anglo-Saxon' is an

5. *Ibid.*, X, 3, 6, 7, 8, 12; XII, 94, 95, 96; TR, *New York*, in *Works*, IX, 398; TR to Frederick Courteney Selous, February 7, 1900, in *Letters*, II, 1175; TR, "Nationalism in Art," in *Works*, XIV, 452. TR, *New York*, in *Works*, IX, 420–21; TR, "Washington's Citizenship," in *Works*, XV, 79; TR, *New York*, in *Works*, IX, 398, 321, 259; TR, "A Naturalist in South America," *Works*, XIV, 528.

6. See Chapter III herein for a discussion of the Anglo-Saxon, Teutonic, and Aryan influences in Roosevelt's thought.

absurd name unless applied to the dominant race in England between the Fifth and the Eleventh Centuries," he wrote in 1905, and two years later he confessed that he was "*very* doubtful" about the existence of an Aryan race.[7] By 1910, when he delivered his lecture at Oxford, "Biological Analogies in History," he was prepared to comment sarcastically that there was "an element of unconscious and rather pathetic humor in the simplicity of half a century ago which spoke of the Aryan and the Teuton with reverential admiration, as if the words denoted, not merely something definite, but something ethnologically sacred; the writers having much the same pride and faith in their own and their fellow countrymen's purity of descent from these imaginary Aryan or Teutonic ancestors that was felt a few generations earlier by the various noble families who traced their lineage direct to Odin, Æneas or Noah."[8]

Perhaps one final example will serve to illustrate the dynamic character of his racial language. As a young historian, steeped in Teutonic racial and historical theory, he had, like most late-nineteenth-century American historians, indulged in scholarly judgments based on exceedingly fine ethnic and racial distinctions. In his first book, *The Naval War of 1812*, the twenty-four-year-old Roosevelt solemnly noted that of all the racial types to be found in Ireland the "Celto-Turanian kern" made the least satisfactory sailor.[9] Thirty years later in a 1912 review of Henry Osborne Taylor's *The Medieval Mind*, Roosevelt chided the great medievalist for his use of outdated racial terminology. Forgetful of his early assessment of the "Celto-Turanian kern" and with characteristic concern for precision of language and anthropological distinctions, Roosevelt noted: "I can only guess at his [Taylor's] reason for calling Attila a 'Turanian'—a word which carries a pleasant flavor of pre-Victorian ethnology, and might just about as appropriately be applied to Tecumseh."[10]

The components of Roosevelt's racial theories thus changed

7. TR to Thomas St. John Gaffney, May 10, 1901, in *Letters*, III, 76; TR to James Brander Matthews, July 20, 1907, *ibid.*, V, 723.
8. TR, "Biological Analogies in History," *Literary Essays*, in *Works*, XIV, 83.
9. TR, *The Naval War of 1812*, in *Works*, VII, 34.
10. TR, "Productive Scholarship," in *Works*, XIV, 342.

over his lifetime. To analyze his racial views without recognizing this dynamic quality presents a distorted picture not only
of what Roosevelt thought but how and with what conceptual
tools he thought.

The critical concept and thus the most important term to understand in Roosevelt's racial lexicon is the word *race* itself.
Historians have either failed to inquire into Roosevelt's understanding of race (and by implication the early-twentieth-century
version of the concept) or they have only partially recognized
that *race* meant significantly different things to Roosevelt than
it does to late-twentieth-century scholars. For example, George
Sinkler in *The Racial Attitudes of American Presidents from
Abraham Lincoln to Theodore Roosevelt*, offered only the observation that Roosevelt was "guilty of using the word race
loosely on occasion,"[11] and one of Roosevelt's most recent biographers incompletely noted that Roosevelt "equated race
with nationality."[12] However, when TR's ideas are placed in
the context of anthropological theory of his time, much of the
confusion about Roosevelt and "race" vanishes.

Upon first inspection, it does appear that Roosevelt used the
term *race* with careless abandon. At various times during his
life, *race* could mean the Aryan race or the Latin race, and national groups such as the Dutch and the Spanish were spoken of
as races. *Race* could identify ethnic groups such as the Scotch-
Irish or might denote a group whose members lived in several
countries. Roosevelt was fond of discussing the French race in
this latter context. He thought the Presbyterian Irish a "stern
and virile race," and he casually referred to a "Kentucky race,"
a "Texas race," or even a "backwoods race" when he wished to
stress some special, historical attribute or virtue. His favorite
term was "the English-speaking race," a politically pregnant
rubric which implied that Britishers, Americans, South Africans, and Australians were yoked in bonds of blood and language and also suggested that those of non-English ancestry,
such as Dutch, could still gain admission into the group which

11. Sinkler, *The Racial Attitudes of American Presidents*, 378.
12. Harbaugh (ed.), *The Writings of Theodore Roosevelt*, 197.

Roosevelt believed was destined to dominate the world. Use of the phrase "English-speaking race" had clear advantages over another term then popular, for Roosevelt could hardly claim membership for himself in an Anglo-Saxon race.[13]

The historian's first impulse might be to dismiss Roosevelt's multitudinous definitions of *race* because of their inconsistency or vagueness. However, period dictionaries, thesauruses, and other specialized works reveal that Roosevelt's usages of *race* found general acceptance. For example, the *Universal Dictionary of the English Language*, published in 1902, listed two principal definitions. Race could be a "lineage, line, family, [or] descent," or it could mean "a class of individuals sprung from a common stock; the descendants of a common ancestor; a family, tribe, nation or people belonging to the same stock." Each of Roosevelt's usages becomes understandable in the context of this definition. Similarly, a period thesaurus indicates the formal acceptability of Roosevelt's usage by including as synonymous for race, the words *nation, ethnology*, and *parent-progeny*.[14]

The ways in which Roosevelt used the term *race* can be grouped into five principal divisions. Early in his life and primarily in his histories he repeatedly used *race* as a broad designation, appropriate to employ when discussing nearly any human group which appeared to possess social, physical, or cultural traits in common. A second general way in which Roosevelt utilized the term was as a national label. Frenchmen belonged to a French race, Germans to a German race, Americans to an American race, and so on. This second level of meaning closely resembled a third which indicated that close ties of a racial nature existed between such peoples as the French and the French Canadians (both members of the French race); the English-speaking race (sharing cultural traits which Roosevelt regarded as racial), or the Latin and Teutonic races, both of

13. For TR's understanding of the links between the Dutch and the English-speaking peoples, see page 57.

14. *Universal Dictionary of the English Language*, III (New York, 1902), 879; Francis A. March, *A Thesaurus Dictionary of the English Language* (Philadelphia, 1902), 850.

which were historical races sharing common pasts as well as physical and behavioral similarities.[15] Roosevelt also defined race on a color basis. At various times he recognized white, red, and black races in North America and also referred to a yellow race as a primary unit of human classification. And finally, Roosevelt conceived of race as representing the principal ethnic divisions of mankind. Roosevelt's fundamental assumptions about race, therefore, were built into a belief system which stressed a plural concept of race, a concept which permitted a significant variety of human groups to be recognized as races.

Although Roosevelt claimed to approach race in a dispassionate, objective manner, his formal terminology was only one aspect of a bifurcated language of race, with a crude idiom always lurking just beneath the surface of the more genteel, theoretical terms. While TR seemed to derive considerable pleasure from the frequent private use of racial and ethnic epithets, he rarely used the terms in public. For Roosevelt, the Irish were "micks," Germans were "Dutchmen," and Italians "dagos," and he referred to the theories of educator Maria Montessori as "a dago adaptation" of Froebel's ideas. The term, however, was something of an umbrella word, for Roosevelt also found it useful to allude to Latin Americans as "dagos." In a similar spirit he referred to the Chinese as "chinks" and the Japanese as "Japs" after the popular usage of the time. Moreover, he used a variety of terms with respect to blacks. Although he scrupulously avoided using the epithet "nigger," preferring "Negro" instead, he frequently spoke of "colored people," "mulattoes," "darkeys," and on rare occasions "quadroons" and "octaroons." The extent of this language and the frequency of its usage indicates the preoccupation with racial differences that Roosevelt and his contemporaries had, but it also suggests that Roosevelt's professed objectivity in matters of race should not always be taken at face value.[16]

15. Other examples of this level of meaning for race included the Slavic and Romantic races and the Hispano-Indian race.

16. TR to Theodore Douglas Robinson, January 22, 1900, in *Letters*, II, 1135; TR to Henry Cabot Lodge, August 20, 1886, *ibid.*, I, 108–109; TR to Thomas R. Lounsbury, November 27, 1911, *ibid.*, VII, 443; TR to Kermit Roosevelt, October 23, 1906,

Although the historical and social roles and the worth and potentiality of these races were determined within a theoretical matrix that blended scientific, anthropological, and historical thought, evolutionary principles provided the crucial intellectual supports for most of this theory. In acknowledging the profound impact of the evolutionary hypothesis, Roosevelt noted that Darwin had "fairly revolutionized thought"[17] and recognized the importance of evolution to studies of natural science and human society. "He who would fully treat of man," Roosevelt said, "must know at least something of biology . . . and especially of that science of evolution which is inseparably connected with the great name of Darwin."[18] Several years later the former president added that "the law of evolution is as unconditionally accepted by every serious man of science to-day as is the law of gravitation."[19]

Although Roosevelt's theoretical speculations about race occurred in a Darwinian context, they were never merely functions of the evolutionary hypothesis. In fact, he dealt selectively with Darwinian dogma, carefully defining his own understanding of evolution, excluding certain ideas and qualifying others. In an 1895 review of Benjamin Kidd's *Social Evolution*, which provided the clearest evidence of young Roosevelt's understanding of social Darwinism, he discoursed at length on evolutionary theory and the applicability of the Darwinian hypothesis to the study of human society. By this time, he had moved away from the highly schematic, holistic ideas that characterized the racial theory of investigation embedded in the first volumes of *The Winning of the West* toward a fuller recognition of the complexity of human experience. The essay reveals young Theodore Roosevelt as a perceptive critic of the attempts to explain human history and human behavior through simplistic Darwinian analogies. In particular, Roosevelt refused to

---

ibid., V, 465; TR to Elihu Root, September 26, 1907, *ibid.*, V, 809; TR to John Hay, July 26, 1904, *ibid.*, IV, 865; TR, *A Book Lover's Holidays in the Open*, in *Works*, IV, 286–93. Also see Chapter V herein.

17. TR, "National Life and Character," in *Works*, XIV, 232.
18. TR, "Biological Analogies in History," in *Works*, XIV, 69.
19. TR, "The Search for Truth in a Reverent Spirit," in *Works*, XIV, 431.

accept the notion that the process of natural selection governed human progress, and he objected to Kidd's assertion that progress was greatest where the "limits" of natural selection were widest and competition keenest. Roosevelt believed that "the rivalry of natural selection is but one of the features in progress." Elaborating upon this point, he argued that other things "being equal," Kidd's statement was relatively correct, but quickly noted that "'other' things never are equal." Moreover, he continued, "in actual life those species make most progress which are farthest removed from the point where the limits of selection are very wide, the selection itself very rigid, and the rivalry very keen." Kidd also erred in arguing that human societies progressed most when reproduction rates were so high that they induced severe competition for scarce means of subsistence or survival itself. If Kidd's argument were accepted, Roosevelt concluded, it would mean that progress had been greatest among "South Italians, the Polish Jews, and the people who lived in the congested districts of Ireland"—all groups whose "progress" did not favorably compare with that of "the dominant strains among . . . the English or Germans."

Competition of the tooth-and-claw variety, a key element in popular Darwinism, did not provide Roosevelt a satisfactory explanation of progress. There should be a "certain amount" of competition, he argued, "a certain amount of stress and strain, but . . . if this competition becomes too severe the race goes down and not up." Furthermore, he added, "the race existing under the severest stress as regards this competition often fails to go ahead as fast even in population as does the race where the competition is less severe." [20] Thus, in a time when fears of race suicide were already present in his mind, he placed a low premium on struggle and natural selection as agents of progress.

> Progress is made in spite of it, for progress results not from the crowding out of the lower classes by the upper, but on the contrary from the steady rise of the lower classes to the level of the upper, as the latter tend to vanish, or at most barely hold their own. In progressive societies it is often the least fit who survive;

20. TR, "Social Evolution," in *Works*, XIV, 108–11.

but on the other hand, they and their children often tend to grow more fit.[21]

Unlike those who subscribed to the Spencerian and Sumnerian points of view, Roosevelt took the general stand that evolution did not necessarily ensure steady progress. For the rest of his life he adhered to the belief that progress was not foreordained and found it a "rather irritating delusion" that "somehow or other we are all necessarily going to move forward in the long run." He admitted, however, a "very firm faith in this general forward movement, considering only men of our own race for the past score or two centuries."[22]

Just as he questioned the Darwinian notion of progress, Roosevelt also continued to doubt various other aspects of Darwinian theory, differentiating, for example, between Darwinism and evolution, and correctly observing that the two were often confounded. Natural selection continued to draw his skepticism with respect to its applications to society and the natural scientific validity of the concept itself. "I suppose that all scientific students now accept evolution, just as they accept the theory of gravitation, or the general astronomical scheme of the solar system and the stellar system as a whole," he wrote James J. Walsh in 1909, "but natural selection, in the Darwinian sense, as a theory, evidently does not stand on the same basis."[23]

Roosevelt's mature statement on evolution is found in his 1910 Oxford University Romanes Lecture. He accepted the invitation, an annual honor reserved for distinguished scientists, with uncharacteristic humility and spent weeks carefully polishing and refining his lecture. His old friend Henry Fairfield Osborn of the Museum of Natural History offered a lengthy critique, and in addition, the president tried out his remarks on several other listeners before he left the White House to travel through Africa in 1909.[24] The lecture, delivered at Ox-

21. *Ibid.*, 112.
22. TR to Arthur James Balfour, March 5, 1908, in *Letters*, VI, 961.
23. TR to James Joseph Walsh, February 23, 1909, *ibid.*, VI, 1535.
24. Henry F. Osborn to TR, December 15, 1908, in Roosevelt Collection, Library of Congress.

ford near the end of his journey, revealed the qualified parallels Roosevelt perceived between human society and nature.

In "Biological Analogies," Roosevelt again rejected interpretations of evolution which emphasized struggle. Although he did not completely exclude struggle as a factor in evolution, he chose to emphasize other evolutionary features, specifically seeking to demonstrate how "races," civilizations, and nations followed the same pattern of life, death, birth, growth and change, of biological species.[25] Cautious as always about the relationship between evolutionary theory in the natural and social worlds, Roosevelt noted that there was "no exact parallelism" between the life cycles of species and those of societies. With admirable circumspection, he wrote: "How far the resemblances between the two sets of phenomena are more than accidental, how far biology can be used as an aid in the interpretation of human history, we cannot at present say."[26] The sweep of history covered such a vast time span that generalizations from evolutionary law should be made carefully, for "throughout this immense period form succeeds form, type succeeds type, in obedience to laws of evolution, of progress and retrogression, of development and death, which we as yet understand only in the most imperfect manner." As knowledge increases, Roosevelt said, "wisdom is often turned into foolishness, and many of the phenomena of evolution which seemed clearly explicable to the learned master of science who founded these lectures, to us nowadays seem far less satisfactorily explained."[27]

Despite these elaborate and oft-repeated disclaimers of the limited usefulness of the Darwinian analogy, several of Roosevelt's key evolutionary concepts emerge from the essay. The primary analogy which he drew between natural history and human history concerned the faunal development of the South American continent. During the tertiary period, Roosevelt contended, "a peculiar and diversified mammalian fauna" made

25. TR, "Biological Analogies in History," in *Works*, XIV, 76–77.
26. *Ibid.*, 69.
27. *Ibid.*, 70–71.

up largely of "rather small species" dominated the South American landscape. But with an "upheaval of land" near the end of the period, a land bridge developed linking the two continents. Across this bridge from the north poured "an inrush of huge, or swift, or formidable creatures which had attained their development in the fierce competition of the arctogeal realm." A "riot of life" followed, during which many of the "smaller, or less capable" of life forms died out, victims of the fierce competition with the northern animals. Others adjusted, however, developing new "bulk" or "armor protection" and thus surviving. A few of these species actually wandered into North America, but more importantly, South American life became dominated by the stronger, North American species. Inexplicably, however, "destruction fell on this fauna," and South America "once again became a land with a mammalian life small and weak compared to that of North America and the Old World" containing only "diminutive representatives of the giants of the preceding era." [28]

Superficially, Roosevelt seemed to be analogizing between conflict in the natural domain and conflict between white North Americans of European stock and the indigenous peoples of South America long isolated from the flow of European history. Certainly Henry Fairfield Osborn interpreted Roosevelt's analogy in that vein. "Your general analogy seems to me correct that we are witnessing a competition between the vigorous races, members of which have been tried out on three continents . . . and the relatively untried races of a long isolated land mass, South America." [29] In this sense it appeared that Roosevelt generally did wish to stress the superior strengths of the northern races and the weaknesses of the tropical groups. Similarly, reference to the inability of northern types to persist in the environment of the Southern Hemisphere alluded to the commonly held belief that northern races could not long endure in the tropics, an interpretation reinforced by other al-

28. *Ibid.*, 74–77.
29. H. F. Osborn to TR, December 15, 1908, in Roosevelt Collection, Library of Congress.

lusions to unhealthy tropical conditions later in the essay. More importantly, however, Roosevelt employed the organic analogy to explain his theory of the spread of "civilization" by the higher races and to reveal the primordial mechanics which characterized that process.

An illustrative example which he frequently used and one which he employed in "Biological Analogies" concerned the folk wanderings of the so-called Teutonic and Nordic races in early European history. During this period of "ethnic overflows from the North" new states were founded in the south of Europe. These were new states in that "part or all of the people composing them were descended from races that hitherto had not been civilized," and they began "through a reflex action" to extend their influence "back into the cold forests from which the invaders had come," just as a few of the new South American faunal types had influenced North American species. Significantly, however, the northern Europeans, unlike the southerners, remained racially pure. "In those communities, unlike the southern communities, there was no infusion of new blood, so that the new civilized nations which gradually developed were composed entirely of members of the same races which in the same regions had for ages lived the life of a slowly changing barbarism." To the east the process had been repeated in the founding of Russia, Roosevelt argued, where a combination of "Scandinavian leaders from the north, and an infiltration of Byzantine culture from the south" combined to "produce the changes which have gradually . . . formed the mighty Russian Empire of today." [30] Thus, according to TR, this basic process of nation formation had its roots in race, evolution, and ethnology, and in the belief that northern racial groups possessed special powers.

If this great law illustrated the birth of nations, another suggested that nations, races, and civilizations did not remain young always. At the far end of the evolutionary continuum lay the specter of racial and national decadence, the fate of those

30. TR, "Biological Analogies in History," in *Works*, XIV, 77–78.

groups who had lost the primary virtues. What was decadence? It had overtaken Rome when "greed and luxury and sensuality ate like acids into the fibre of the upper classes." The "average citizen" at the same time "had lost the fighting edge," and the empire had become depopulated.[31] A similar fate befell the Dutch "race" which had lost neither "vitality" nor the power of reproduction, but had succumbed to "the fatal weakness . . . so common in rich, peace-loving societies where men hate to think of war as possible, and try to justify their own reluctance to face it by high-sounding moral platitudes, or else by a philosophy of shortsighted materialism." These debilitating effects could sometimes be reversed, Roosevelt claimed, for "Holland and Italy teach us that races that fall may rise again."[32]

Roosevelt's understanding of evolution had a special quality best explained by reference to the intellectual milieu of the period. As George Stocking has observed in *Race, Culture, and Evolution*,[33] a self-conscious group of neo-Lamarckian anthropologists professed a particularized set of ideas about race and evolution which differed sharply from Sumnerian and Spencerian interpretations of the two intimately related concepts. To a remarkable extent, Roosevelt's ideas paralleled those of the neo-Lamarckians. The great principle of neo-Lamarckianism, the inheritance of acquired characteristics, could be applied in many areas of scientific and social speculation and investigation. A significant portion of American social scientists during the years 1890–1915 counted it as central to their understanding of race, culture, and evolution. The acquired-characters doctrine could explain the evolution of human races and societies; for some, the principle was the "major mechanism of the evolution of the mind."[34]

As Stocking has shown, Lamarckianism figured in many areas

31. *Ibid.*, 86–87.
32. *Ibid.*, 88.
33. George W. Stocking, *Race, Culture, and Evolution: Essays in The History of Anthropology* (New York, 1968). See the essays entitled "The Persistence of Polygenist Thought in Post-Darwinian Anthropology" and "Lamarckianism in American Social Science, 1890–1915."
34. *Ibid.*, 238–40.

of turn-of-the-century racial theory. The concept of adaptation, for example, was at the heart of the question of race formation. Moreover, Lamarckianism did not stress the immutability of racial characteristics which many physical anthropologists regarded as essential to an understanding of the nature of race; instead the theory emphasized the power of environment as opposed to the importance of heredity. Thus the racial past of any people was a "bio-social" past, one which combined elements of biological heredity with characteristics acquired through the influence of environment and culture. Even physical features might be modified by social processes, argued leading social scientists such as Paul Reinsch. For Lamarckian social scientists, as for Roosevelt, race did not play a principal role as "an independent causal variable in the explanation of social phenomena." As Stocking has cogently observed, "racial heredity, though it might help to explain certain social phenomena, was itself ultimately the implicitly Lamarckian product of social and environmental forces."[35]

For Lamarckians, complex cultural traits could be acquired, carried, and transmitted in the "blood" of "races" from generation to generation. The major problem facing these social scientists of the early twentieth century "was not their domination by notions of biological or racial *determinism*, but rather their obfuscation by a vague sociobiological indeterminism, a 'blind and bland' shuttling between race and civilization."[36] Distinctions between race and culture were hazy, and social scientists as well as talented amateurs like Roosevelt often "shuttled" back and forth between the two concepts across the Lamarckian bridge which linked them.

Theodore Roosevelt was a committed neo-Lamarckian. Nearly every aspect of his racial belief system meshes with Lamarckian theory and can be properly understood only if one bears in mind the profound Lamarckian influence upon his mind. It is at the very base of his racial theory and his entire social philosophy. In his first major theoretical statement on race, Roose-

35. *Ibid.*, 244.
36. *Ibid.*, 265.

velt left no doubt that he was a Lamarckian. Human progress, Roosevelt wrote, was "due mainly to the transmission of acquired characters, a process which in every civilized state operates so strongly as to counterbalance the operation of that baleful law of natural selection which tells against the survival of some of the most desirable classes." Responding to those who attacked the validity of the concept, Roosevelt observed that "the view that acquired characteristics cannot be inherited . . . is hardly worth serious refutation."[37] Like so many of the neo-Lamarckians, he had been stung by the Mendelian theories propounded by August Weismann. The theory of the continuity of germ plasm seemed especially outrageous to Roosevelt and many other neo-Lamarckian race theorists who were repelled by the deterministic, illiberal character of Weismann's ideas. The German geneticist's discoveries seemed to be foreclosing the theoretical validity of the acquired-characters doctrine, the equipotentiality of races, and the important Lamarckian concept of use and disuse. Moreover, his ideas indicated that the force of the environment upon the development of races and societies was minimal if not nonexistent, a condition completely unacceptable intellectually to the neo-Lamarckians and especially to Roosevelt, who held firmly to the notion that environment could be of great importance not only to the strengthening and perpetuation of a race but also to race formation itself.

As late as 1912 Roosevelt, in a self-conscious affirmation of the strength of his Lamarckian convictions, dismissed Weismann's contentions and restated his belief in the limited applicability of the Darwinian hypothesis to social conditions. To Francis H. Herrick, professor of biology at Western Reserve University, Roosevelt wrote that the work of Ernst Haeckel, which posited a philosophical and religious system based on Darwinian theory, was unscientific "extreme dogmatism." More importantly, he also condemned the unscientific "acceptance as facts of Weismann's extreme theories."[38] Like most of his

37. TR, "National Life and Character," in *Works*, XIV, 249.
38. TR to Francis H. Herrick, January 15, 1912, in *Letters*, VII, 478.

social scientist contemporaries, Roosevelt held fast to the doctrines of Lamarckianism all through the lively controversy over the theory's validity. However, in "Biological Analogies in History," he had diplomatically conceded to the Oxford dons that indeed "scientific men of most note now differ widely in their estimates of the relative parts played in evolution by natural selection, by mutation, [and] by the inheritance of acquired characteristics," speculating that there were other "forces at work which our blinded eyes wholly fail to apprehend." [39]

Nevertheless, in his last major essay, written eight years after the Oxford lecture, Roosevelt reaffirmed his Lamarckianism. In a lengthy review of Henry Fairfield Osborn's *The Origin and Evolution of Life*, he discounted British experiments which sought to dispel the idea of acquired characteristics. "Most scientific men nowadays disbelieve in the inheritance of acquired characteristics," the aging Roosevelt acknowledged, but he warned against making facile distinctions between the inheritance of acquired characteristics and the "inheritance of an acquired pathological condition," which the British scientists had attempted to make. Great care should be taken, he added, before investigators "lay down laws of sweeping application to thought and conduct." [40]

Throughout his life, Roosevelt had incorporated many features of Lamarckianism into his thought. He was, for example, a unilinear evolutionist arguing that all races had descended from a single ancestor, a conceptual element of Lamarckianism which supported the notion of equipotentiality. He argued in 1910 that "phylogenetically, each animal now living must necessarily trace its ancestral descent back through countless generations, through eons of time, to the early stages of the appearance of life on the globe." [41] "Phylogenetically," he added, "the line of ancestral descent must be of exactly the same length for every existing individual, and for every group of individuals, whether forming a family or a nation." [42] Never impervious

39. TR, "Biological Analogies in History," in *Works*, XIV, 71.
40. TR, "The Origins and Evolution of Life," in *Works*, XIV, 36–37.
41. TR, "Biological Analogies in History," in *Works*, XIV, 71–72.
42. *Ibid.*, 77.

to the latest scientific thought, however, he began late in life to
turn over in his mind the concepts of parallel and divergent evolution, and tilted with the notion that "*energy, and not form*"
lay at the beginning of the evolution of life.[43]

Although he had mildly emphasized physical characteristics
of race in his earlier celebration of the physical characteristics
of the frontiersmen, Roosevelt came to discount the importance
of physiognomy as an indication of racial ability or potential.
He would never have subscribed to some of the more bizarre
theories of racial determinism, which, for example, posited the
character and ability of entire races upon anthropometry. In
addition, Roosevelt like most neo-Lamarckians found much of
the physical anthropology which served as a basis for the harsh
racial determinism of the day to be highly suspect. Again he attempted to steer a middle course between two extremes by re-
jecting the theories of William Z. Ripley, who held that heredity governed physical form absolutely, and those of William
Ridgeway, who argued that environment controlled "racial
or physical form" absolutely. But, like other Lamarckians, he
tended paradoxically to accept a general classification of races
on the basis of skull type, occasionally wandering off into a
discussion of theories of heredity with respect to unions between different skull types. But even in this area Roosevelt,
ahead of his time, noted what he perceived to be the limited
worth of studying human types according to whether they possessed "brachycephalic," "dolichocephalic," or "mesatoce-
phalic" skulls. "On any other theory," he wrote Osborn, "I do
not know how to account for the fact that in any extensive collection of skulls from America and Europe it is absolutely impossible to draw the line separating one type from the other,
the gradations being imperceptible from the brachycephalic to
the dolichocephalic."[44]

Speculating upon the development of physical types in 1914,
he displayed an inchoate awareness of differences between culture and race. In Europe there had been "on the whole steady
development in physical type—sometimes the type itself grad-

43. TR, "The Origins and Evolution of Life," in *Works*, XIV, 31.
44. TR to H. F. Osborn, December 21, 1908, in *Letters*, VI, 1435.

ually changing, while sometimes it was displaced by a wholly different type of wholly different blood." Parallel to this development a "corresponding development in cultural type" had occurred, a phenomenon "often wholly unrelated" to the change in physical type.[45] Thus, Roosevelt underscored his belief that physical characteristics could not be related directly to what he dimly perceived as cultural development—a conceptual distinction on his part which set him in the very forefront of early-twentieth-century anthropological theory.

This was not always the case, however, for Roosevelt throughout most of his life, like nearly every Lamarckian, blithely mixed the cultural with the racial. This is particularly the case with respect to the stages-of-development scheme which he applied to races, nations, and civilizations. Reflecting to some extent the influence of eighteenth- and nineteenth-century social thinkers, historians, and philosophers who saw mankind developing in clear-cut stages, Roosevelt developed a scheme to explain stages of development. Races, for example, proceeded from savagism, a state of disorganized chaos, to barbarism, a stage where the military "virtues" were developed, into a third stage which blended the best of military virtues with love of order and race fecundity, the sum of which represented "social efficiency." Beyond this stage was a fourth level where the great "virile virtues" diminished and were replaced by love of ease, softness, willful sterility, too much emphasis upon the contemplative life, and too much stress upon material possessions. The fifth and last stage was decadence or death.[46]

Races in their prime possessed certain key characteristics. "All the great masterful races," Roosevelt wrote, "have been fighting races, and the minute that a race loses the hard fighting virtues, then, no matter what else it may retain, no matter how skilled in commerce and finance, in science or art, it has lost its proud right to stand as the equal of the best." "Success," Roosevelt wrote, "is for a mighty race, in its vigorous and mas-

---

45. TR, *A Book Lover's Holidays in the Open*, in *Works*, IV, 155.
46. The stages theory appears in virtually all of Roosevelt's writings. For its fullest exposition, see "The World Movement," in *Works*, XIV, 258–85.

terful prime."[47] "Unless we keep the barbarian virtues," he told the psychologist G. Stanley Hall in 1899, "gaining the civilized ones will be of little avail."[48] And, of course, cowardice in a race was an unpardonable sin.[49]

Roosevelt's Lamarckian orientation provided the raw materials for the development scheme. While his subscription to the idea of unilinear evolution provided the intellectual basis for acceptance of a notion of progress through consecutive, successive stages, his adherence to the doctrine of acquired characteristics simplified his explanation of how races and individuals could obtain different characteristics and then pass them along to the next generation. Acceptance of the idea of use-disuse allowed him to stress the necessity for practicing the virile virtues, lest they be lost. A Lamarckian deemphasis on the importance of heredity to physical type and stress on the power of the environment to change this aspect of racialness permitted him to posit even the alteration of physical manifestations of race.

The Lamarckian idea was also compatible with one of the most powerful themes in Roosevelt's life, the belief that society could be changed by altering the social environment. To reform a society which permitted the unregulated distribution of contaminated food and dangerous drugs, to extirpate corruption in politics, or to create social conditions which protected revered American institutions like the family meant to TR that individuals and groups might through environmental change acquire desirable characteristics which could be transmitted from generation to generation. Neo-Lamarckianism thus interacted not only with Roosevelt's racial thought but with his beliefs about the efficacy of reform as well.

All societies, civilizations, and races stood somewhere in Roosevelt's developmental format. Each could move upward by acquiring characteristics which comported with the "virile

---

47. TR, *The Winning of the West*, in *Works*, XII, 92.
48. TR to Granville S. Hall, November 29, 1899, in *Letters*, II, 1100; TR to G. F. Becker, July 8, 1901, *ibid.*, III, 112.
49. TR, "Our Neighbors, the Ancients," in *Works*, XIV, 54.

virtues," and each could slide backward by acquiring undesirable traits or losing the desirable ones. The worth of a race and its future could be determined by assessing its virtues, its faults, and its position on the savagism-decadence continuum. Since racial traits were inheritable through the process of Lamarckian evolution, all races could theoretically improve and could even overcome decadence. The stages-of-development scheme then was largely open-ended, full of possibility and chance.

Within this broad framework of language and scientific and social scientific theory Theodore Roosevelt considered race and its importance to human history and experience. From the days when, as a young historian, he drank deeply of Teutonic-origins theory and Anglo-Saxonism until the time of his death when he was more concerned with scientific and theoretical notions, ideas of race were his constant companions.

CHAPTER III

History and the Anglo-Saxon Tradition

Theodore Roosevelt belonged to the group of "gentlemen historians" who presided over the writing of American history in the last quarter of the nineteenth century. Like Henry Adams, John Bach McMaster, Moses C. Tyler, and James Ford Rhodes, all of whom produced major works on American history, Roosevelt researched and wrote history with a powerful concern for themes of national unity and greatness in the style of the talented amateurs who had long dominated the American historical craft. Unlike those who would later dominate the scene, these scholars at various times pursued other careers and established their historical reputations outside the academy.

From 1881 through 1895, the period of Roosevelt's greatest scholarly activity, a quiet revolution occurred within the historical craft. Young men trained in the German graduate schools to be professional historians attempted to study history "scientifically" and concentrated much of their effort in searches for the origins of societal institutions. Scholars on both sides of the Atlantic shared a fascination for these ideas. In England, historians William Stubbs and Edward A. Freeman advanced theses which argued that the origins of English civilization could be traced to Teutons who had developed proto-democratic political forms in the forests of Germany during the early Middle Ages. Such ideas lent themselves easily to parallel notions concerning the racial superiority of Germanic peoples and found eager advocates in the United States where the Teutonic origins theory became a powerful theme in American historical scholarship. While variations on the concept abounded, most American historians leaned heavily on the researches of Herbert Baxter Adams, professor of history at Johns Hopkins University and the foremost American advocate of Teutonic theory.

Roosevelt also became fascinated by the apparent links between Teutonic practices and American governmental forms, and went beyond many of the new historians and discovered a vast reservoir of historico-racial characteristics bequeathed Americans by the Teutons and Anglo-Saxons. Like many "old-stock" Americans in the late nineteenth century, Roosevelt looked to the Anglo-Saxon and Teutonic traditions for evidence of genealogical and racial sanctity. From his youth, he had partaken of the fund of racial, historical, and literary beliefs which collectively constituted Anglo-Saxonism and Teutonism, praising the historical Anglo-Saxon and Teuton, lauding the English-speaking race as the nineteenth-century embodiment of those "racial" types and discovering in the American frontiersman all of the best traits of both. For Roosevelt, however, these concepts were not rigid, abstract scientific ideas but quasi-mystical theories which had their principal sources in the Anglo-American, Germanic, and northern European historico-literary traditions rather than in the domain of physical anthropology and natural science. Still, his version of Anglo-Saxonism and Teutonism comfortably meshed with his Lamarckianism; environment and heredity could operate symbiotically to permit the emergence of an American type which combined the best racial characteristics of the Anglo-Saxon and Teutonic pasts with the environmentally induced improvements of the American frontier. The clearest evidence of this phenomenon and of the fundamental racial mechanism which Roosevelt perceived as operative in human affairs occurs in his historical writing.

An affinity for history marked Roosevelt's thought throughout his life. From the publication of *The Naval War of 1812* in 1882 to the presidency of the American Historical Association thirty years later, he made use of the dominant conceptions of historical scholarship and the historian's craft in scholarly and nonscholarly pursuits alike. Roosevelt's model historian was Francis Parkman. So much did he admire the Parkman style that he dedicated *The Winning of the West* to the older scholar whose "capacity for wide and deep research," and accuracy in establishing details awed the young New Yorker. Yet he most highly prized Parkman's perception that the truly significant event of American history was the conquest of the continent by the white race, and the struggle over "which branch of the white race should win for itself the right to make this conquest."[1] The future American president, following Parkman's lead, strongly emphasized not only the racial aspects of conflict between whites and Indians, but also viewed the entire breadth of the American past through a racial lens. With constant, almost compulsive attention to underlying racial themes, he researched, analyzed, and synthesized the raw materials of history.

The force of race in history occupied a singularly important place in Roosevelt's broad intellectual outlook. In fact, race provided him with a window on the past through which he could examine the grand principles of historical development. None of human history really meant much, Roosevelt believed, if racial history were not thoroughly understood first. Although his fascination with racial matters may have stopped short of determinism in the sense that he did not believe that racial character absolutely foreordained behavior, he clearly perceived past human experience in a racial framework.

Nordicism, Anglo-Saxonism, and Teutonism are among the strong racial themes which can be traced through the nearly forty years of his wide-ranging historical studies, but the fullest expositions of these ideas occur in his four principal histories, *The Naval War of 1812, Thomas Hart Benton, Gouverneur Morris*, and his four-volume chronicle of the frontier *The Winning of the West*. In these books, the preponderant themes are palpably white supremacist.

Roosevelt produced his first book, *The Naval War of 1812*, at age twenty-three, less than a year after his graduation from Harvard. Long recognized as a standard work in the field of military history, the study combines the themes of romantic na-

1. Theodore Roosevelt, "Francis Parkman's Histories," in *Works*, XIV, 287.

tionalism and white supremacy which characterized much of the Anglo-Saxon tradition. Elements of Teutonic and Anglo-Saxon theory present in the book include the concept of blood (the idea of inheritable race traits), a complex assortment of racial stereotypes deriving from the blood concept, and the notion that a particular branch of the Teutonic peoples, the English race, had a unique historical destiny. Early in the book Roosevelt disclosed a major theme that Americans and Englishmen shared a common racial character superior to other non-Teutonic stocks. The war itself, he argued, was an unfortunate but still heroic family squabble, the lessons of which could not be learned without the insight that Americans and Britishers were two substantially similar branches of the great English race whose close kinship accounted for the war's virtual stalemate.[2]

Although the two "races" had unfortunately clashed, either "race" could be proud of "the many feats of fierce prowess done by the men of their blood and race."[3] After all, the racial composition of the two was virtually the same. Both had assimilated at various times in history the blood of other Teutonic peoples and in America the original English stock had actually been recapitulated. The three elemental strains in the English "race," German, Irish, and Norse, had in America recombined "in about the same proportions" as originally. Therefore, the English stock, "mainly Teutonic, largely Celtic . . . with a Scandinavian admixture," persisted in North America in very pure form. Although this stock undoubtedly remained purest in New England, the young historian argued, the New Jersey and New York Dutch had so thoroughly interbred with the pure stock that at the time of the war they were "by race nearer to the true old English of Alfred and Harold than are, for example, the thoroughly anglicized Welsh of Cornwall."[4]

In spite of the effort to demonstrate the integrity of his own racial stock and to show that through recapitulation American

2. TR, *The Naval War of 1812*, in *Works*, VII, 24–26.
3. *Ibid.*, 304.
4. *Ibid.*, 24–26.

blood was more English than the modern English could boast, Roosevelt stressed basic racial similarities in the two peoples. American and Englishman shared certain inherited traits similar to those of other Teutonic peoples, but of higher quality. Both were "bold and hardy, cool and intelligent, quick with their hands and showing at their best in an emergency."[5] According to the Lamarckian historian, one of the few differences could be found in the fact that the American did have an edge in fighting skill, due mainly to the influences of the American environment.[6]

High assessments of the English and Americans allowed Roosevelt to rate other races in comparison. One way to decode his estimate of the merits of non-English groups at this early stage of his life is to examine the stereotypes which appear in the book. The standard by which he judged all the war's combatants was the "cool, gritty, American Jack," who was "shrewd, quiet, and . . . rather moral."[7]

Although Roosevelt found most "races" of the Teutonic and Anglo-Saxon group to be able fighters, he made subtle distinctions even within this charmed circle. The Irish sailor, for example, performed nearly as well as the American and Englishman—"if he came from the old Dano-Irish towns of Waterford, Dublin, and Wexford, or from the Ulster coast." His cousin, whom Roosevelt dubbed the "Celto-Turanian kern," apparently lacked the genetic configuration necessary for good mariners and "did not often appear on shipboard." The fierce Norsemen whose racial qualities he admired intensely were deemed excellent sailors and fighters.[8]

Other races contrasted sharply with the American. "The Creole soldiers," he noted, "came of a race whose habit it has ever been to take all phases of life joyously" but on the morning of the Battle of New Orleans a "dark undercurrent of fierce anxiety" tempered the happy racial disposition of these mixed-blood

5. *Ibid.*, 33–34.
6. *Ibid.*, 33n.
7. *Ibid.*, 30–31.
8. *Ibid.*, 34.

descendants of the original French settlers of Louisiana. Like the Creoles, Portuguese and Italians made comparatively poor wartime showings. As in the case of most hot-blooded Latins, "they were treacherous, fond of the knife, less ready with their hands, and likely to lose either their wits or their courage when in a tight place."[9]

American Indian and black outcasts in Teutonic theory occupied a relatively insignificant place in this racial chronicle of naval warfare. Foreshadowing his point of view in *The Winning of the West* ten years later, Roosevelt saw a dying Indian race which stood helpless before the mighty crush of the American frontiersman. He did not dwell extensively upon the racial character of blacks in this book, but noted only that "quite a number" served as marines.[10] Thus, deeply influenced by Teutonic mythology, Roosevelt worked out his explanation of the fighting and outcome of a provincial war within a network of racial theory in which his version of Teutonic and Anglo-Saxon theory, modified somewhat to fit the historical setting, accounted for the behavior of entire races of Americans, northern Europeans, and southern Europeans. That Roosevelt could seriously argue for such fine differences among various ethnic and regional groups is not so much a commentary upon his personal predilection for ascribing racial traits to virtually any human group as it is a reflection of the rococo character of late-nineteenth-century racial theory and ethnology. Such observations found general acceptance among both serious scholars and amateurs.

Six years after *The Naval War of 1812* Roosevelt published *Thomas Hart Benton*. In this book, the young New Yorker emphasized the Teutonic leitmotif even more thoroughly. The 1887 biography of the Missouri senator is hardly a biography at all but rather a hastily written statement of Roosevelt's personal views and values poured out during his longest pilgrimage into the Dakota wilderness. In *Benton* Roosevelt extended and refined his racial explanation of American history, posited

9. *Ibid.*, 446, 34.
10. *Ibid.*, 260–61.

the existence of a distinct American race, and philosophized about the political and racial future of the nation.[11] While environmental influences had elevated Roosevelt's American of 1812 slightly above the Englishman, the "stern and hard surroundings" of life on the first frontier hardened the transplanted European of *Benton* into a "peculiar and characteristically American type," a race whose bloodlines Roosevelt believed had remained virtually unchanged through the first 250 years of American history. All of the romantic traits associated with Teutonism now appeared in this new type. Capable of the "fiercest intensity of purpose," the hardy frontiersmen conquered the West in an amoral fashion which Roosevelt floridly romanticized.[12] They planned western conquest, he wrote in a bow to Nordicism, "with very little more idea of there being any right or wrong in the matter than so many Norse Vikings might have felt."[13]

Roosevelt viewed this Nordic-Teutonic kaleidoscope of western expansion as one gigantic race settlement which loomed "infinitely more momentous" in comparison to the petty territorial disputes of Europe. But the young scholar perceived internal differences in the intensity of this struggle, differences which he naturally interpreted in a racial framework. Along the frontier of the middle border, for example, the struggle required tremendous strength in contrast to the conquest of California, which had entailed only the subduing of "stunted and scanty native races." In another of a seemingly endless series of historical parallels Roosevelt likened this settlement of the Mississippi Valley to the "tribe movements of the Germanic peoples in times past," and saw a very striking similarity to the movement "by which the Juttish and Low Dutch sea-thieves" had conquered Britain.[14] The middlewestern frontiersmen responsible for this feat constituted a "most war-like race" and had accomplished their great task precisely because they shared

11. TR, *Thomas Hart Benton*, in *Works*, VIII.
12. *Ibid.*, 4–5.
13. *Ibid.*, 42.
14. *Ibid.*, 5.

the same blood and belonged to the same race.[15] Above all else, they had "strong, virile" traits with no trace of softness. "A race of masterful spirit," they were "stern, rude, and hard . . . Americans through to the very heart's core."[16]

In one of the book's major digressions Roosevelt discussed enthusiastically the conquest of Texas, utilizing a capacious Teutonic literary simile which erupts frequently throughout the book. He likened the Texas adventure to the conquests of the "Norse sea-rovers" and described the Texans as men with virtues and faults like those of Nordic barbarians. "Restless, brave and eager for adventure, excitement and plunder; they were warlike, resolute and enterprising; they had all the marks of a young and hardy race, flushed with the pride of strength and self-confidence." Reflecting the powerful Darwinian influence of his time, he reported with great relish how the settlers had looked upon the possessions of weaker races as their "natural prey." Roosevelt's Texans had no greater scruples "than a ship-load of Knut's followers" a thousand years before. Moreover, they could count on assistance in time of need from their blood kin east of the Mississippi just as "Rolf's Norsemen on the seacoast of France [could] rely confidently on Scandinavian help in their quarrels with their Karling overlords."

The apotheosis of this virile, amoral nineteenth-century Nordic was Sam Houston. All of the manly traits typical of a young race reposed in Houston, who, if the effusive Roosevelt is to be believed, stood "mighty in battle and crafty in council, with his reckless, boastful courage and his thirsts for changes and risks of all kinds." Houston was an "old world Viking" with a career "as picturesque and romantic as that of Harold Hardraada himself."[17]

Essentially, the seizure of Texas from the Mexicans constituted a fulfillment of white racial destiny, the "domineering, masterful spirit and bitter race prejudices" of the white frontiersmen explaining the displacement of the Mexicans, who

15. *Ibid.*, 6, 8.
16. *Ibid.*, 16, 17.
17. *Ibid.*, 132–33.

belonged to a race completely alien "in blood, language, religion and habits of life." "It was out of the question," Roosevelt wrote, to expect Americans to "submit to the mastery of the weaker race." Whatever reasons might be advanced to explain the conquest, he insisted that "the real reasons were to be found in the deeply marked difference of race and in the absolute unfitness of the Mexicans then to govern themselves." [18]

These heavily racial themes appeared again in Roosevelt's next book, a biography of founding father Gouverneur Morris, published in 1888.[19] In *Morris* Roosevelt extended and refined his version of Anglo-Saxonism and Teutonic theory and perceived American racial characteristics in a Teutonic framework which allowed him to rhapsodize about the qualities responsible for the successful establishment of the American nation. Whereas he had emphasized racial fighting qualities in *Benton* and *The Naval War of 1812*, the thirty-year-old historian now stressed another aspect of Teutonic theory, the inherited ability for self-government. The men who attended the American Constitutional Convention represented a "type" which had frequently appeared "among the liberty-loving nations who dwelt on the shores of the Baltic and the North Sea." Men destined to govern others as well as themselves, they represented the type "in its highest and most perfect shapes," but genius alone did not explain a greatness which sprang from "the union of strong, virile qualities with steadfast devotion to a high ideal." Above all, Roosevelt declared, "they possessed that inestimable quality, so characteristic of their race, hard-headed common sense." [20]

While these demigods might have inherited few faults, other European stocks by contrast had acquired grievous flaws. The young historian derisively condemned "swinish German kinglets who let out their subjects to do hired murder, and battened on the blood and sweat of the wretched beings under them." [21]

18. *Ibid.*, 131–32.
19. TR, *Gouverneur Morris*, in *Works*, VIII.
20. *Ibid.*, 375–77.
21. *Ibid.*, 337–38.

The French were a decadent race, lacking in self-restraint, "volatile," and "debauched."[22] Fortunately, Gouverneur Morris, the erstwhile subject of the book, had inherited less egregious Gallic traits such as an "alert vivacity and keen sense of humor" and enough Teutonic blood to render him correct on political matters and to enable him to see "with unusual clearness, that each people must have a government suited to its own individual character, and to the stage of political and social development it had reached." Moreover, Morris, aware like his biographer that races only slowly acquired the instinct for self-government, "would have dismissed with contemptuous laughter the idea of those Americans who at the present day believed that Anglo-Saxon democracy can be applied successfully to a half-savage negroid people in Hayti."[23]

Scarcely one year after the publication of *Gouverneur Morris* Roosevelt completed the first volume of his epic of American expansion in *The Winning of the West*.[24] Full of confidence for the future of the white races, he synthesized and systematized for the first time the themes scattered throughout his first three histories. In a letter to Frederick Jackson Turner he confessed that his principal concern lay not in developing an institutional history of western expansion but in examining the type of men who were responsible for the winning of the West. "My aim is especially to show who the frontiersmen were and what they did," Roosevelt wrote Turner after the latter had favorably reviewed the first volume.[25] Later, to reiterate the point, he wrote Turner, who had praised the work for its Anglo-Saxon emphasis, that "in *type* the men [of the West] were the same." By "type" Roosevelt of course meant racial type.[26]

The lengthy introduction to *The Winning of the West* reveals the extent of his convictions regarding the importance of racial differences. The young historian's interests ensured that he would approach any historical project with an eye to race, but his special passions for western expansion and racial theo-

22. *Ibid.*, 414.
23. *Ibid.*, 280, 372–73.
24. TR, *The Winning of the West*, in *Works*, Vols. X, XI, and XII.
25. TR to Frederick Jackson Turner, April 10, 1895, in *Letters*, I, 440.
26. TR to Frederick Jackson Turner, April 26, 1895, *ibid.*, I, 446.

ries demanded that he consider the former in terms of the latter. In the introduction he explained not only the course of American history in racial terms, but also delineated a broad philosophy of history which included key principles derived from his understanding of the dynamics of race in history. *The Winning of the West*, considered against such a background, becomes as much a racial saga as an explanation of American history.

According to Roosevelt the spread of the "English-speaking peoples" throughout the world's "waste spaces" amounted to "the most striking feature in the world's history."[27] While men who belonged to this "race" had tamed vast areas of the earth, the conquest of North America remained the most significant aspect of the worldwide movement. The extension of the rule of the English-speaking "race" over alien lands should not be viewed, however, as "mere conquest" but rather as the broadest and most rapid instance of "race expansion" in the world's history. The roots of this "race expansion" were found in the forests of Germany.

In ancient times the Germanic peoples had steadfastly resisted the absorption and loss of their culture to the Roman legions advancing from the south, finally prevailing on "the day of the slaughter by the Teutoburger Wald, when the legions of Varus were broken by the rush of Hermann's wild warriors." By successfully staving off this amalgamation with Rome, Germans established an important historical precedent for other groups to follow in preserving their peculiar composition and heritage. Moreover, the persistent Germans after an interlude of several hundred years "went forth from their marshy forests ... to conquer" and for centuries "swarmed out of the dark woodland east of the Rhine and north of the Danube." As their force increased, the movement was joined by "their brethren who dwelt along the coasts of the Baltic and the North Atlantic." Eventually, every land bowed to the "war-like prowess of the stalwart sons of Odin," acknowledging "the sway of kings of Teutonic or Scandinavian blood."[28]

Drawing many lessons from the German experience, Roose-

27. TR, *The Winning of the West*, in *Works*, X, 3.
28. *Ibid.*, 3, 4.

velt stressed above all the preservation of racial purity and cultural integrity. Yet even the Germans ultimately failed to heed their own example and soon displayed an inability to prevail fully over conquered peoples. Winning battles offered no particular problem but the inability of the conquerors to outbreed their new subjects flawed their conquests and shortened the duration of Teutonic rule. Subject peoples began quickly to absorb them. "The Dane in Ireland became a Celt; the Goth of the Iberian peninsula became a Spaniard; Frank and Norwegian alike were merged into the mass of Romance-speaking Gauls." Despite the ability of the German tribes to conquer Europe they failed to expand permanently the territorial limits of Germany and "the sway of the German race" precisely because they failed either to remove or physically absorb subject peoples. On the contrary, argued Roosevelt, the German conquests primarily served to strengthen the character of the conquered peoples. While the conquerors provided leaders and place names, altered the system of justice, and "interpolated a few Teutonic words in the Latin dialects" of the subdued peoples, they were unable to preserve the German race stock in the face of the overwhelming "mass of their subjects." "As a result," Roosevelt concluded, "the mixed races of the south—the Latin nations as they are sometimes called—strengthened by the infusion of northern blood, sprang anew into vigorous life, and became for the time being the leaders of the European world." [29]

Roosevelt's emphasis on breeding and the power of the northern "blood" to strengthen the presumably weaker southern races foreshadowed a principal cornerstone of his racial theories, the idea that a race must maintain a very high fertility rate to avoid losing its identity to a people of superior breeding powers. This theory suggested that any race must absorb alien stocks at home in order to preserve racial integrity and would have to absorb or displace conquered peoples in order to maintain extraterritorial gains. In Roosevelt's view of history, the conquest of Britain by individuals of Germanic stock provided

29. *Ibid.*, 4–5.

a significant example of a successful implementation of this principle and an exception to the general experience of the conquering Germanic races. Britain, Roosevelt wrote, "was destined to be of more importance in the future of the Germanic peoples than all their continental possessions original and acquired, put together."

The racial and national roots of the British could be traced to a special branch of the Teutonic race for which young Roosevelt had an understandable affinity. "The day when the keels of the Low Dutch sea-thieves first grated on the British coast was big with the doom of many nations," the Dutch-descended Roosevelt wrote. As a result of the actions of the Teutonic germ carriers, "there sprang up in conquered southern Britain, when its name had been significantly changed to England, that branch of the Germanic stock which was in the end to grasp almost literally world-wide power, and by its overshadowing growth to dwarf into comparative insignificance all its kindred folk." These Low-Dutch seamen possessed all of the admirable racial traits and even had acquired a certain virile lawlessness which Roosevelt admired. The descendants of these "hard-rowing, hard-fighting henchmen," he approvingly noted, "now hold in their hands the fate of the coming years."[30]

The Dutch sea-thieves had guaranteed the English "race" a "perfectly continuous history" because in conquering Britain they did not simply overrun subject territories as the Germans had done on the continent. Instead of being absorbed themselves they "displaced" the natives. Unlike the Germans, who eventually had allowed the "subject-races" to assimilate them, the Low-Dutch sea-thieves Roosevelt proudly noted, "slew or drove off or assimilated the original inhabitants." "Unlike all the other Germanic swarms, the English took neither creed nor custom, neither law nor speech, from their beaten foes"; thus purity of culture and race survived.[31]

Roosevelt placed special emphasis on the principle of race purity and defined it in genealogical terms which rested on his understanding of historical racial development. His need to

30. *Ibid.*, 5–6.
31. *Ibid.*, 7.

establish links for Americans with the Teutonic past represented a romantic effort to identify the American tradition of white supremacy with the heroic deeds and conquests of the Germanic tribes, in particular the Low-Dutch whom he regarded as having a racially pure, clear line of descent eventuating in the English-speaking peoples. Frenchmen, Spaniards, and others of the Latin races, on the other hand, had no clear heritage. He argued that the history of these peoples did not really begin until after the "great Teutonic wanderings" were over, "whereas that of the Germanic peoples stretches back unbroken to the days when we first hear of their existence." Therefore the Latins had no clear patrimony, their mixed heritage being much less desirable than that of the Germanic peoples. "It would be hard to say," Roosevelt declared in a digression on the bastardy of the Latin races, "which one of half a dozen races that existed in Europe during the early centuries of the present era should be considered as especially the ancestor of the modern Frenchman or Spaniard." Roman blood had infused that of the original inhabitants, and the "Frankish and Visigothic invasions" added yet another strain. Unlike descendants of the racially legitimate Germanic tribes, the Latin races, of dubious parentage, took "portions of their governmental system and general policy from one race, most of their blood from another, and their language, law, and culture from a third." "It would be hard to say," Roosevelt stressed, "whether Vercingetorix or Caesar, Clovis or Syagrius, has the better right to stand as the prototype of a modern French general." The case of the "average" Englishman, American, or Australian, was different. If he wished "to recall the feats of power with which his race should be credited in the shadowy dawn of its history," he could look proudly to the "glories of Hengist and Horsa, perhaps to the deeds of Civilis the Batavian, or to those of the hero of the Teutoburger fight, but certainly to the wars neither of the Silurian chief Caractacus nor of his conqueror, the after-time Emperor Vespasian."[32]

32. *Ibid.*, 6, 7.

But should any reader believe that an understanding of racial bloodlines could be regarded as having doubtful importance to an appreciation of American history, Roosevelt advised:

All this is not foreign to American history. The vast movement by which this continent was conquered and peopled cannot be rightly understood if considered solely by itself. It was the crowning and greatest achievement of a series of mighty movements, and it must be taken in connection with them. Its true significance will be lost unless we grasp, however roughly the past race-history of the nations who took part therein.[33]

With the heritage of the American people clearly delineated and with the proper stress laid upon knowing their past "race-history," Roosevelt now explained how the conquest of America had been an historical and racial recapitulation of the conquest of England by the Low-Dutch "sea-thieves." Just as his understanding of ancient racial movements recapitulated the life cycle of biological species, so too the winning of the West recapitulated the taking of Britain.

The English, joined by other European "races," reached across the Atlantic for a great period of expansion and conquest just as the Germanic tribes had swarmed out of the forests of central Europe. Eventually, however, Europeans imported African slaves into the New World, an occurrence which Roosevelt decried because it jeopardized the reenactment on American shores of the process by which England had been won, it offered an obstacle to the unimpeded flow and development of white civilization, and it threatened racial purity. As a result of this "folly," he wrote, "throughout the continent, we . . . find the white, red, and black races in every stage of purity and intermixture." This intermixture had advanced to the point that in some areas "the lines of cleavage of race are so far from coinciding with the lines of cleavage of speech that they run at right angles to them."[34]

Like many nineteenth-century race theorists Roosevelt be-

33. *Ibid.*, 8.
34. *Ibid.*, 9.

lieved that language was associated with race and accepted the principle that it behooved a race to preserve its linguistic integrity, if race purity were to endure. Moreover, a common language was necessary to "race unity" and for at least this reason racial intermixing was undesirable. Preserving the language, as the English had done for a thousand years, assured the continuation of a rich and productive culture which could be transmitted to the next generation, but the language could not have prevailed had the early invaders of England allowed themselves to have been assimilated by the more numerous natives. In similar fashion, any race seeking to extend its influence should heed the example of the English in preserving the linguistic aspect of racialness and should be aware that the earlier Teutonic wanderings had failed partially because of an inability to maintain linguistic ascendancy. Here history offered still another lesson.

As Roosevelt had earlier stressed, England's greatness could also be traced to the foresight of the "Low-Dutch sea-thieves" in not permitting their blood to be watered down by inferior, indigenous races of old Britain. Instead, and in contrast to other Germanic tribes then wandering through Europe, they had killed or driven off the natives. This supreme principle of Roosevelt's racial theory of history had been observed in the American recapitulation of the English experience. Mixing with the North American aborigines would have stultified the development of English and American civilization; it was necessary to displace inferior races. The history of Spanish conquest offered an example of the consequences of failing to heed this principle. In North America, the Spaniards "simply sat down in the midst of a much more numerous aboriginal population," much as the Romans had in the countries of southeastern Europe centuries before. The price to be paid for such an error, Roosevelt cautioned, was extermination of the civilization of the conquering race by the superior breeding powers of the conquered. "Though the ordinary Spaniard of today speaks a Romance dialect," Roosevelt noted, "he is mainly of

Celto-Iberian blood; and though most Mexicans and Peruvians speak Spanish, yet the great majority of them trace their descent back to the subjects of Montezuma and the Incas." When the English arrived in America, they avoided the error of the Spanish and emulated the conquering style of their ancestors, "displacing" the local population instead of intermixing with them.[35] For Roosevelt, this point had immense significance:

> It is of vital importance to remember that the English and Spanish conquests in America differed from each other very much as did the original conquests which gave rise to the English and Spanish nations. The English had exterminated or assimilated the Celts of Britain, and they substantially repeated the process with the Indians of America; although of course in America there was very little, instead of very much, assimilation. The Germanic strain is dominant in the blood of the average Englishman, exactly as the English strain is dominant in the blood of the average American. Twice a portion of the race has shifted its home, in each case undergoing a marked change, due both to outside influence and internal development; but in the main retaining, especially in the last instance, the general race characteristics.[36]

The establishment of English superiority in North America thus rested upon preserving the "general race characteristics." A contemporary problem suggested how important it was to preserve these traits. In South Africa, Roosevelt pointed out, "the English are confronted by another white race which it is as yet uncertain whether they can assimilate." What was "infinitely more important," however, was that a large native population stood in the way of English control of South Africa, one "with which they cannot mingle, and which neither dies out nor recedes before their advance." Ever prepared with a historical example which bore some resemblance to a contemporary situation, Roosevelt prophesied that: "It is not likely, but it is at least within the bounds of possibility, that in the course of centuries the whites of South Africa will suffer a fate akin to

35. *Ibid.*, 9–13.
36. *Ibid.*, 12.

that which befell the Greek colonists in the Tauric Chersonese, and be swallowed up in the overwhelming mass of black barbarism." [37]

In America and Australia "the English race" had already begun the "enjoyment of its great inheritance," but the American struggle had required special strength and endurance because of the racial nature of the opposition encountered. Settlers in Australia had only to overcome natives of a "low type" whose resistance hardly differed from that of "an equal number of ferocious beasts." In America, a succession of contests had been fought with groups strong enough to challenge but not to overcome the white frontiersman. Americans, in their struggle to tame the continent, encountered European "races" as well as the Indians who though "far more to be dreaded than the Zulus or even the Maoris" managed only for a while to stay the "oncoming white flood." Because the racial contest had been fiercer for the American than for his Australian or Canadian counterpart he had emerged the stronger and more confident "race." [38]

Roosevelt stressed that the Americans who had accomplished this feat belonged to a race distinctive both biologically and culturally. In doing so, he briefly explained his understanding of the process of assimilation in America.

Moreover, it is well always to remember that at the day when we began our career as a nation we already differed from our kinsmen of Britain in blood as well as in name; the word American already had more than a merely geographical signification. Americans belong to the English race only in the sense in which Englishmen belong to the German. The fact that no change of language has accompanied the second wandering of our people, from Britain to America, as it accompanied their first, from Germany to Britain, is due to the further fact that when the second wandering took place the race possessed a fixed literary language, and, thanks to the ease of communication, was kept in touch with the parent stock. The change of blood was probably as great in one case as in the other. The modern Englishman is descended from a Low-

37. *Ibid.*, 14.
38. *Ibid.*, 14–17.

Dutch stock, which, when it went to Britain, received into itself an enormous infusion of Celtic, a much smaller infusion of Norse and Danish, and also a certain infusion of Norman-French blood. When this new English stock came to America it mingled with and absorbed into itself immigrants from many European lands, and the process has gone on ever since. It is to be noted that, of the new blood thus acquired, the greatest proportion has come from the Dutch and German sources, and the next greatest from Irish, while the Scandinavian element comes third, and the only other of much consequence is French Huguenot. Thus it appears that no new element of importance has been added to the blood. Additions have been made to the elemental race-strains in much the same proportion as these were originally combined.[39]

The young historian desired the best of both worlds. Maintaining that a distinctly American race existed, he nevertheless could show that it was principally an improvement on the old but admirable English stock which itself had descended from the "Low-Dutch stock." Recombining the original race stocks on American shores added a nice touch to his recapitulatory explanation of American history. Because no new elements had been added to the blood in significant proportions, Americans could expect to enjoy through the reinfusion of new blood the inherited race traits of the old stock as well as the characteristics acquired as a result of the frontier struggle.

But the principal thrust of Roosevelt's work was the winning of the western frontier and he now attempted to relate directly his historico-racial theories to the internal dynamics of American expansion where conquest had occurred within two specific phases, each with racial implications. While the old Southwest had been subdued "by the people themselves, acting as individuals," the government had made possible the peopling of the Northwest through its guarantees of protection. Settlers there merely took possession of the land. In the old Southwest, however, the actions of a particular "type" had accounted for the development of civilization along lines unimpeded by the formal organization which marked the Northwest experience.

39. *Ibid.*, 19–20.

Roosevelt had glorified this "type" in his earlier histories, but now he completed the parallel to the earlier conquest of England, accentuating its similarity to the conquest of the Southwest and emphasizing the racial heritage of the southwesterner, who was, it would seem, a sort of "Low-Dutch sea-thief" reincarnate.

> The warlike borderers who thronged across the Alleghanies [*sic*], the restless and reckless hunters, the hard, dogged, frontier farmers, by dint of grim tenacity, overcame and displaced Indians, French, and Spaniards alike, exactly as, fourteen hundred years before, Saxon and Angle had overcome and displaced the Cymric and Gaelic Celts. They were led by no other commander; they acted under orders from neither king nor congress; they were not carrying out the plans of any far-sighted leader. In obedience to the instincts working half-blindly within their breasts, spurred ever onward by the fierce desires of their eager hearts, they made in the wilderness homes for their children, and by so doing wrought out the destinies of a continental nation.[40]

Because the southwesterner belonged to the American race, he naturally possessed all of the characteristics of that group, but Roosevelt also found in him a blend of virtues and faults which raised him to a very high rank in the racial hierarchy. Like the "sea-thieves," the "backwoods race" had "good and evil traits in their character such as naturally belonged to a strong, harsh, and homely race, which with all its shortcomings, was nevertheless bringing a tremendous work to a triumphant conclusion."[41] Roosevelt saw the experience of the southwesterner and indeed the entire frontier experience as occurring in a literal state of nature and in the breast of this primeval Anglo-Saxon of the frontier the "instinct" for self-government throbbed. Although the southwesterners had come to the Southwest without protection from the government, they soon intuitively began to organize on their own.

Organizing for protection and establishing a system of justice posed no serious problem. American customs and traditions

40. *Ibid.*, 22–25.
41. *Ibid.*, XI, 231.

eased the transition into some sort of political organization, but the Anglo-Saxon "race-capacity for self-rule" which resided within the frontiersmen made the difference.[42] In Tennessee, for example, the settlers' establishment of a government could be attributed to the "unconscious reproduction of the laws and customs of the old-time court-leet, profoundly modified," as Roosevelt explained, "to suit the peculiar needs of backwoods life, the intensely democratic temper of the pioneers, and, above all, the military necessities of their existence."[43] Here his belief that the Teutonic and Anglo-Saxon "races" possessed an inherited ability to construct governmental forms was very clear and revealed the extent to which he had imbibed the Teutonic theories of race and government.

Perhaps remembering his resolve to study the racial "types" responsible for these wondrous works and having already established the existence of a new American race, Roosevelt proceeded to study the specific ethnic composition of the frontiersman in an attempt to distinguish finely the relative capabilities of various groups. On the frontier, where conditions tested individual fiber, certain stocks were better suited for the tasks of extending the line of civilization. The backwoodsmen, he concluded, were of "mixed race; but the dominant strain in their blood was that of the Presbyterian Irish—the Scotch-Irish as they were often called."[44] He felt that the Presbyterian-Irish (as distinguished from the Catholic Irish whom he did not greatly admire) had received short shrift from historians, who had awarded full credit to the "Round-head and the Cavalier for their leadership in our history" and had not "wholly realized the importance of the part played by that stern and virile people, the Irish whose preachers taught the creed of Knox and Calvin." Although they had "mingled with the descendants of many other races, they nevertheless formed the kernel of the distinctively and intensely American stock who were the pioneers of our people in their march westward." Not satisfied

42. *Ibid.*, 188.
43. *Ibid.*, 192.
44. *Ibid.*, 96.

with establishing that the Presbyterian Irish occupied special importance in the racial composition of the American frontiersmen, Roosevelt also sifted the lineage of the Scotch-Irish themselves in order to understand more clearly the development of the West. A tenacious, vigorous people, their ancestry could be traced mainly to the "Scotch Saxons and the Scotch Celts," though many had English or French Huguenot blood. "Quite a number," Roosevelt allowed, were "of true old Milesian Irish extraction."[45]

Roosevelt found the final distillation of the Anglo-Saxon and Teutonic race traits in the Kentuckian. The Kentuckian of the early Southwest had "looked with bold and greedy eyes at the Spanish possessions, much as Markman, Goth, and Frank had once peered through their marshy woods at the Roman dominions." The Kentuckian possessed virtues "proper to a young and vigorous race," the kind of virile aggressive racial "faults" which Roosevelt admired and thought necessary for racial dominance. "Trammelled by few misgivings as to the rights of the men whose lands he coveted," this latter-day Teuton "felt that the future was for the stout-hearted and not for the weakling."[46]

The future president believed that under the conditions of frontier warfare the "young and vigorous race" of frontiersmen often temporarily regressed to a lower level of human development. Two thousand years of the development of "merciful humanity" could be lost as the great frontier task unfolded. But although he professed a distaste for the savagery of the frontier conflict, he could scarcely disguise his fascination with frontier bloodletting. "It is primeval warfare, and it is waged as war was waged in the ages of bronze and of iron. . . . It is a warfare where no pity is shown to non-combatants, where the weak are harried without ruth, and the vanquished maltreated with merciless ferocity." Roosevelt concluded that "a sad and evil feature of such warfare is that the whites, the representatives of civilization, speedily sink almost to the level of their barbarous foes in point of hideous brutality."[47] Nevertheless, al-

45. *Ibid.*, 96–97.
46. *Ibid.*, XI, 329.
47. *Ibid.*, 276.

though he unconvincingly professed disapproval of this violence, the fighting character of the frontiersmen remained the quality which Roosevelt most admired in the American race. This trait, of course, had been handed down through countless generations from the early Teutonic wanderers to the hardy "Southwesterner," the repository of all of the virtues and faults of Teutonic character. To lose the fighting instinct would mean that the American tended toward decadence.

Roosevelt also obviously derived great satisfaction from displaying his mastery of Teutonic mythology which allowed him to allude with great flourish to the familiar and the obscure in that set of ideas. Yet even if some of Roosevelt's racial rhapsodizing is attributed to this penchant for literary bombast, the evidence in *The Winning of the West* and in Roosevelt's other histories overwhelmingly suggests that the future president accepted an interpretation of history based upon the Anglo-Saxon and Teutonic complex.

Still Roosevelt did not always accept so uncritically all of the tenets of Anglo-Saxonism. By 1905, with much of Teutonic theory passé, he had decided that no Anglo-Saxon "race" really existed, and declared that if he were to rewrite his histories he would use neither the terms *Scotch-Irish* nor *Anglo-Saxon*.[48] In addition, he had doubts about the worth of Aryanism, another racial theory closely related to Anglo-Saxonism. While he had used the term *Aryan* in some of his early reviews, his reading of de Michelis' *L'Origine degli Indo-Europei* convinced him that *Aryan* more properly belonged to the linguistic and not the racial realm. In a letter to Benjamin Ide Wheeler, president of the University of California, he noted that he had been very impressed by de Michelis' grasp of the "relationships between languages and races," and particularly with his assertion that "Aryan is a linguistic and not a biological term."[49] Moreover, three years later in 1907 he declared himself "*very* doubtful" that an Aryan race existed.[50]

If Roosevelt eventually eschewed some of the labels of Anglo-

48. TR to Thomas St. John Gaffney, May 10, 1901, in *Letters*, III, 76.
49. TR to Benjamin Ide Wheeler, May 11, 1904, *ibid.*, IV, 795.
50. TR to James Brander Mathews, July 20, 1907, *ibid.*, V, 723.

Saxonism and related ideologies which pervaded his histories, he preserved the substance of its most central tenets. His celebration of the heritage, exploits, and destiny of the "English-speaking race" continued largely unabated throughout his life and scarcely differed from his earlier lauding of Anglo-Saxons and Teutons. In this "race" Roosevelt saw cultural and linguistic unity as the essence of racialness, the "English-speaking race" providing an effective conceptual substitute for the more traditional Anglo-Saxon idea. In his history of New York he rapturously recounted how few had grasped "the grandeur of the movement by which the English-speaking race was to spread over the world's waste spaces." It had become, Roosevelt wrote, "the mightiest race on which the sun has ever shone."[51] The concept of an English-speaking "race" could thus be effectively utilized to stress traditional themes of white supremacy in America and throughout the world and in this sense became the vehicle for Teutonic and Anglo-Saxon dogma which Roosevelt had consumed. It also provided a racial standard by which nonwhites would be judged.

51. TR, *New York*, in *Works*, IX, 321.

CHAPTER IV

Indians

The image of the American Indian in Theodore Roosevelt's mind was a product of his cultural heritage, his own speculations about the racial character of the Indians, and his actual encounters with native Americans in the West. This image, appearing for the most part in his early formal writings, included a variety of racial and cultural characteristics which he ascribed to the American aborigine. Despite his personal encounters with Indians, the red man became more and more an abstraction, an image which moved stealthily and furtively through Roosevelt's writings, always lurking somewhere in the background and assuming in the end the status of a symbol of brutality, fierceness, and strength. The conquest of this formidable foe signified for Roosevelt the triumphal greatness of the American struggle for the West, the superior power and potency of the white frontiersman.

Roosevelt considered Indians and Indian character in several distinct frames of reference. As a historian, he interpreted the racial character and role of the "savage" Indian in relation to the foreordained, relentless advance of white "civilization." Although much of the information which he marshaled about the Indian in this context was an elemental part of his cultural heritage, the tribes he observed on his forays into the West contributed to the image of the Indian which he carefully constructed in his histories. As a politician Roosevelt devised solutions to "the Indian problem," and finally, Roosevelt developed beliefs about Indians as a result of his nonpolitical, nonscholarly activities as a soldier in Cuba during the Spanish-American War and as a traveling reporter-anthropologist in his post-presidential years.

Roosevelt believed that the savage state represented the lowest level of existence to which humans could belong, and he assigned the historical Indian, the image of the Indian in his histories, to the savage level. The Indian was compared, unfavorably, with the atavistic frontiersman whom TR occasionally celebrated for his savage-like virtues; yet he saw the gulf between the two as vast: "They [the Indian and the frontiersman] represented two stages of progress, ages apart; and it would have needed many centuries to bring the lower to the level of the higher." [1] Roosevelt conceived of savagism in relation to those features of existence which he considered civilized. Indians clearly did not possess love of order and social efficiency, key ingredients of Roosevelt's view of civilization, but they did enjoy some of the manly virtues—the capacity to breed well and fight well, for example. Despite these admirable traits the essential Indian remained a savage.

Typical of his estimate of the general state of civilization among Indians were his observations about the Algonquins in *The Winning of the West*. The Algonquins of the Northwest, Roosevelt explained, were "savages, not merely barbarians." Not as far along on the scale of civilization as the tribes of the South, these aborigines were huntsmen, "ruder in life and manner than their Southern kinsmen," and "less advanced toward civilization." Even they, however, were more civilized than the almost entirely nomadic plains Indians. [2]

Although Roosevelt's evaluation of Indian racial nature was almost totally adverse, he did find some tribes more nearly compatible with the cherished values of white civilization. The Cherokees, "a bright intelligent race, better fitted to follow the 'white man's road' than any other Indians" occupied a very high echelon in Roosevelt's aboriginal hierarchy. [3] That tribes of Indians differed greatly Roosevelt realized, but he applied this concept in a manner that permitted him to make very broad judgments about Indian racial character. "Not only do Indians

1. TR, *The Winning of the West*, in *Works*, XII, 105–106.
2. *Ibid.*, X, 64–65.
3. *Ibid.*, 51–52.

differ individually," he wrote in *Ranch Life and the Hunting Trail*, a chronicle of his Dakota adventures, "but they differ as tribes."

> An upper class Cherokee is nowadays as good as a white. The Nez Perces differ from the Apaches as much as a Scotch laird does from a Calabrian bandit. A Cheyenne warrior is one of the most redoubtable foes in the whole world; a "digger" Snake one of the most despicable. The Pueblo is as thrifty, industrious, and peaceful as any European peasant, and no Arab of the Soudan is a lazier, wilder robber than is the Arapahoe.[4]

Considered within his broader framework of ethnic prejudices, these telling comparisons of Indians indicate the relatively crude manner in which Roosevelt constructed his anthropology of Indians. Despite occasional concessions which reveal an awareness of some differences among Indians, broad generalizations abound in Roosevelt's writing which reveal the utter contempt he had for the Indian as a racial type. His approach to the Indian was one of almost entirely unmitigated censure only slightly relieved by admiration for the Indian's fighting abilities.

Roosevelt was thoroughly convinced that Indians displayed social and cultural traits which directly reflected their inferior station as compared to the white, civilized world. An "inhuman love of cruelty for cruelty's sake" characterized "the red Indians above all other savages." So insidious was the Indian's love of barbarity that it moved the young TR to observe that "the hideous, unnameable, unthinkable tortures practised by the red men on their captured foes, and on their foes' tender women and helpless children, were such as we read of in no other struggle hardly even in the revolting pages that tell the deeds of the Holy Inquisition." Anyone who had ever visited an encampment of "wild Indians" and "had the misfortune to witness the delight the children take in torturing little animals [would] admit that the Indians's love of cruelty for cruelty's sake cannot possibly be exaggerated." Indian adults trained

---

4. TR, *Ranch Life and the Hunting Trail*, in *Works*, IV, 486.

their children so that when they matured they would "find their keenest pleasure in inflicting pain in its most appalling form." To stress further the savage nature of the Indian, Roosevelt declared that "among the most brutal white borderers a man would be instantly lynched if he practised on any creature the fiendish torture which in an Indian camp either attracts no notice at all, or else excites merely laughter." In the process of white justice, then, apparently lay the distinctions which the future president saw between savagism and civilization.[5]

Roosevelt believed that the American experiences on the western frontier had not revealed an Indian substantially different from those whom the first colonists had encountered. A pattern for all white-Indian conflicts had emerged on the first frontier where once formidable Indian tribes had been reduced to "a horde of lazy, filthy, cruel beggars always crowding into their [the settlers'] houses, killing their cattle, and by their very presence threatening their families."[6] Thus, the Indian after defeat retained his despicable traits but was shorn of any respectability which his fighting prowess had given him. The frontiersmen "barely considered an Indian as a human being." They knew the warrior was not a "creature of romance" but "filthy, cruel, lecherous, and faithless." Although an admirable quality sometimes appeared in the braves, these occasions were seldom. Similarly, the Indian in peacetime remained a "lazy, dirty, drunken beggar, whom they [the frontiersmen] despised, and yet whom they feared; for the squalid, contemptible creature might at any moment be transformed into a foe whose like there was not to be found in all the wide world for ferocity, cunning, and bloodthirsty cruelty."[7]

Even these extreme deprecations of Indian character, however, were exceeded by Roosevelt's literary rendition of the much-discussed savage penchant for strong drink. Describing the typical conditions surrounding the signing of a treaty between red and white afforded an opportunity to promote the

---

5. TR, *The Winning of the West*, in *Works*, X, 78 and 78n.
6. TR, *New York*, in *Works*, IX, 243.
7. TR, *The Winning of the West*, in *Works*, XI, 8.

historical vision of the Indian as a voracious consumer of whiskey. In *The Winning of the West*, for example, Roosevelt speculated that most Indian treaty signings resulted directly from an immediate desire to acquire the goods white men proffered as inducements. Among these "earnest" goods was, of course, whiskey. "They [the Indians] were especially anxious for spirits, for they far surpassed even the white borderers in their crazy thirst for strong drink." As evidence for this claim Roosevelt adduced the treaty council declaration of a Chippewa spokesman. "We have smelled your liquor and it is very good; we hope you will give us some little kegs to carry home," allegedly said the spokesman of a party of Chippewas from the upper Great Lakes. Many other fire-water consuming braves crowd the pages of Roosevelt's chronicle of western expansion. These "frank savages," he concluded, "uttered what was in the minds of most of the Indians who attended the councils held by the United States commissioners. They came to see what they could get by begging, or by promising what they had neither the will nor the power to perform."[8]

Only when he judged that a group had begun to absorb white ways did he qualify his estimate of the debauched and irredeemable Indian character. For example, those Indians who had progressed sufficiently to accept Christianity deserved special consideration. When a group of "peaceful and harmless" Indian converts to the religion of the Moravians were brutally massacred by white frontiersmen in an unprovoked attack, he pronounced the actions of the pioneers "utterly abhorrent." Yet Roosevelt's estimation of Indian character was so low that he had little difficulty in explaining even the murder of these Indians who had only partially acclimated themselves to white civilization. While senseless, willful murders such as these should have been punished, he admitted, the "extraordiary conditions of life on the frontier must be kept in mind before passing too severe a judgment."[9]

Although convinced like many nineteenth-century Ameri-

8. *Ibid.*, 265.
9. *Ibid.*, 6–8.

can thinkers of the degeneracy of the Indian and quite prepared
to censure him, Roosevelt did not accept two other distinct
ways of regarding the Indian. Unlike those Americans who
viewed the Indian with a mixture of censure and pity, Roosevelt concerned himself little over savages who did not embrace
the ethic and values of white society, and he had great contempt for the nineteenth-century cult which revered the Indian as noble savage, as a man-beast in whom savagism and
nobility of character were subtly blended. The only major virtue which Theodore Roosevelt's thoroughly ignoble savage
possessed was the capacity for great oratory. Like Thomas Jefferson, who found the speeches of Chief Logan comparable to
the "whole orations of Demosthenes and Cicero," Roosevelt
succumbed to the stereotype of the Indian as great orator and
testified to the eloquence of Cornplanter, the Algonquin chief.
Although his admiration for Cornplanter's oratory never overcame his disdain for the Indian's more unlovely traits, the
chief's "speeches showed . . . in a high degree, that loftiness of
courage, and stern, uncomplaining acceptance of the decrees
of a hostile fate, which so often ennobled the otherwise gloomy
and repellent traits of the Indian character."[10] True, Roosevelt
admitted, chiefs like Cornplanter and Logan were occasionally "capable of deeds of the loftiest and most sublime hero-
ism" yet even these finest examples of Indian character were
at times "cruel monsters or drunken good-for-nothings" whose
"meaner followers had only such virtues as belong to the human wolf—stealth, craft, tireless endurance, and the courage
that prefers to prey on the helpless, but will fight to the death
without flinching if cornered."[11]

Roosevelt saw the principal justification for Indian genocide
in the foreordained, inevitable "mighty crush" of westward
advancing white civilization. All red men who impeded the
flow of white progress would fall victim "to the ferocity of the

10. Quoted in Winthrop Jordan, *White over Black: American Attitudes Toward
the Negro, 1550–1812* (Chapel Hill, 1968), 477–78; TR, *The Winning of the West,* in
Works, XI, 266.
11. TR, *The Winning of the West,* in *Works,* XI, 8.

race to which it did not belong." Yet Roosevelt knew that Indians could be ferocious too and because he admired fighting
prowess as a racial trait, he could express at least some admiration for their warring abilities. But this presented a discomfort-
ing intellectual problem. How best could one reconcile admiration for the fighting qualities of a race while concurrently
despising its social traits? Roosevelt's solution of the problem
involved him in a paradox. He would interpret the low and
mean Indian as a tragic figure, inalterably a victim of foreordained white progress, destined like the original Britons to be
"displaced" by whites as prescribed in the opening chapter of
The Winning of the West. If the white advance were to be heroic, and if the white frontiersman were to be judged an able,
virile fighter in the idealistic mold Roosevelt cast for him, then
the foe must be a redoubtable warrior too.

Upon close examination it appeared to TR that the struggle
for the North American continent had been especially heroic,
even more impressive than all other triumphs of the English-
speaking race. Unlike Australia where the aborigines were of
such "low type" that they resisted only slightly more than "an
equal number of ferocious beasts," the conquest of North America had involved the subduing, displacing, and removal of
"powerful, warlike tribes." [12] In the United States, the foes had
been even more imposing than in Canada, where according to
Roosevelt the primary obstacle to white domination had only
been "a singular race of half-breeds, with a unique semicivili-
zation of their own." The American Indian, almost totally un-
affected by the infusion of French blood which had domes-
ticated his Canadian cousins, remained a feral creature who
possessed the finest fighting qualities of any savage anywhere.
Moreover, the American Indian proved to be not only the fiercest of foes but also remarkably adaptable to new techniques of
fighting which whites had introduced, and soon became "accustomed to the newcomers' weapons and style of warfare." Indians were "the most formidable savage foes ever encountered

12. *Ibid.*, X, 15.

by colonists of European stock," and "far more to be dreaded than the Zulus or even the Maoris." They fell back before the "oncoming white flood" only after "fierce and dogged resistance." A less imposing foe might have submitted more easily and thus diminished the "race-importance" of western conquest.[13] To characterize broadly the American Indians as the severest foe ever faced by colonizing Europeans and to emphasize that the English-speaking peoples had prevailed over them when Latin races (the French and Spanish) had not, enabled Roosevelt to glorify in the highest terms possible the conquest of the territory which would become the United States. By concentrating upon the fighting abilities of Indians in general he had elevated the savage to the role of tragic victim of the white advance to the Pacific.

The conflict between red and white remained principally a racial struggle. Just as the racial qualities and capacities of the old-stock whites explained the success of the American frontier experience, so too these traits accounted for the defeat of the savage. In Roosevelt's view, the pioneers had accomplished a task of great "race-importance" in killing off the Indians, a weaker and inferior race. Because the whites had represented the vanguard of civilization, Roosevelt reasoned, their actions should not be judged "by standards which would only be applicable in civilized townships and parishes." The mission of taking the land surpassed all other consideration. "Whether the whites won the land by treaty, by armed conquest, or, as was actually the case, by a mixture of both, mattered comparatively little so long as the land was won. It was all-important that it should be won for the benefit of civilization and in the interests of mankind."[14] Because of the great racial importance he attached to the winning of the West, Roosevelt had early reached the conclusion that the extermination of Indians must be approached with little regard for traditional morality. His forays into the American West in the early 1880s and his admiration for the works of historian Francis Parkman were of spe-

13. *Ibid.*, 16–17.
14. *Ibid.*, XI, 274–75.

cial importance in the development of his rationale for Indian displacement.

Living in Dakota Territory five years or so after Sitting Bull's victory at Little Big Horn gave Roosevelt an opportunity to observe firsthand the American Indian and to absorb some of the local lore about the "savage." Soon after his return to the "civilized" East, the young cowboy-aristocrat published his observations of Indian character and his assessment of Indian-white relations. Relations between the two were "rarely pleasant," he observed, each side having a right to "complain" of bitter wrongs. Although he conceded that "many" frontiersmen were "brutal, reckless, and overbearing" and that "most" Indians were "treacherous, revengeful, and fiendishly cruel," Roosevelt recalled witnessing white outrages against the Indian which deserved condemnation. Indian atrocities, on the other hand, were so egregious that they made him "almost feel that not a single one of the race should be left alive." The major problem, he observed with unconscious irony, was "the tendency on each side to hold the race, and not the individual responsible for the deeds of the latter." [15]

But if the state of Indian-white relations produced any moral dilemma at all in Roosevelt's mind with respect to the inevitable subjugation of the red man, his broader view of American history provided the antidote for brief lapses into sentimentality. The "conquest of this continent by the white race" and the subjugation of the "original red lords of the land" was the issue of transcending importance. Roosevelt found reassurance and a model for his views in the works of Parkman.

Parkman showed his real worth as a historian in "his treatment of the Indians." In particular, Roosevelt admired the perspective which the aging historian brought to his work, perspective gained from visiting the scenes of great Indian-white battles but also from having "lived among the Indians themselves no less than [among] the white borderers." Roosevelt could have been thinking of himself when he praised Parkman

15. TR, *Ranch Life and the Hunting Trail*, in *Works*, IV, 484–86.

for his fieldwork and for knowing firsthand the "Indian character and the character of the white frontiersman." The older
scholar was not a "special pleader for either race" but a historian who "sets out facts as they are, blind neither to the fickle-
ness, treachery, and inhuman cruelty of the red men, nor to the
lawlessness, brutality, and ungovernable greed of the whites."
As might be expected, Roosevelt reached precisely the same
conclusion as Parkman—that the Indian was the victim of the
destiny of a superior race.[16] "In its results, and viewed from
the standpoint of applied ethics," Roosevelt wrote, "the conquest and settlement by the whites of the Indian lands was
necessary to the greatness of the race and to the well-being of
civilized mankind."

> It was as ultimately beneficial as it was inevitable. Huge tomes
> might be filled with arguments as to the morality or immorality of
> such conquests. But these arguments appeal chiefly to the culti-
> vated men in highly civilized communities who have neither the
> wish nor the power to lead warlike expeditions into savage lands.
> Such conquests are commonly undertaken by those reckless and
> daring adventurers who shape and guide each race's territorial
> growth. They are sure to come when a masterful people, still in
> its raw barbarian prime, finds itself face to face with the weaker
> and wholly alien race which holds a coveted prize in its feeble
> grasp.[17]

Although Roosevelt's convictions about the destiny of the
white race predetermined his historical judgment of the United
States government's Indian policy, a dim sense of the gross un-
fairness of that policy pushed him toward attempts to explain
away the Indians' just grievances. These efforts resulted in
some exceedingly contrived rationalizations. He acknowledged
that the Cherokees and the Seminoles had suffered "terrible
injustice."[18] While it had been "a cruel grief and wrong" to
evict the Cherokees from Georgia in the 1830s, it would have
been worse to keep them there deprived of much of their land

16. TR, "Francis Parkman's Histories," in *Works*, XIV, 286–94.
17. TR, *The Winning of the West*, in *Works*, XI, 388–89.
18. *Ibid.*, X, 90n.

and in a state of inferiority to white "civilization."[19] The government had been wise to indemnify fully the "savages" and
to transport them west of the Mississippi thereby solving "the
Indian problem so far as the old States were concerned." Thus
Roosevelt could rationalize that removal "on the whole did not
in the least retard the civilization of the tribe," since the Indians had been "fully paid for [their] losses." If Roosevelt's approval of paying the Cherokees for their lands was inconsistent
with his general view that such treaty making had little genuine
worth or with his notion that Indians had no right to claim title
to the land, it scarcely bothered him, for he proudly noted that
the Cherokees had been paid as much for their lands as the
United States had paid for Florida and Louisiana combined.[20]
In the case of the Seminoles Roosevelt conceded that they
probably had been induced to leave Florida by "fraudulent
representations," but they had agreed and then "declined to
fulfill their agreement," thus bringing on a bitter war. Even
from TR's point of view, there was little in the long and bloody
Seminole War "to which an American can look back with any
satisfaction."[21]

Although "cruel wrongs" had indeed been perpetrated on
the Cherokees, Seminoles, and "peaceful and unoffending"
tribes like the Nez Perce, the future president wished to make
it abundantly clear that, far from condemning American policy
toward the red man, he warmly applauded it. Even a tragedy
like the Sand Creek Massacre, where Colonel J. M. Chivington ordered the murder of 450 men, women, and children, was
"in spite of certain most objectionable details . . . on the whole
as righteous and beneficial a deed as ever took place on the
frontier."[22] After all, from Roosevelt's perspective a war against
savages was the "most ultimately righteous of wars,"[23] and in
the final analysis, the Indian policy advocated by most western men, although it "worked harshly" on occasion and caused

19. TR, *Thomas Hart Benton*, in *Works*, VIII, 44.
20. *Ibid.*, 127–29.
21. *Ibid.*, 157.
22. *Ibid.*
23. TR, *The Winning of the West*, in *Works*, XI, 275.

"a certain amount of temporary suffering" was "really more just and merciful, than it would have been to attempt following out any of the visionary schemes which the most impracticable Indian enthusiasts are fond of recommending."[24]

Roosevelt expended considerable energy defending American attitudes toward the Indians and attacking "enthusiasts" of a "visionary" policy like Helen Hunt Jackson and George W. Manypenny. These "purely sentimental historians" simply did not understand frontier conditions. Manypenny's book *Our Indian Wards* Roosevelt contemptuously dismissed as "a mere spiteful diatribe against various army officers," whereas he argued that Mrs. Jackson's *A Century of Dishonor* should be regarded more seriously since it was "capable of doing more harm." Roosevelt praised Mrs. Jackson for attempting to prevent additional injustices against the Indian, but he condemned the book itself since it was not "technically honest," calling it "beneath criticism" as a history and "thoroughly untrustworthy from cover to cover." Mrs. Jackson's book, Roosevelt noted, had achieved a certain status among the "large class of amiable but maudlin fanatics" and "foolish sentimentalists" who "not only write foul slanders about their countrymen, but are themselves the worst possible advisers on any point touching Indian management."

The focus of the one-sided dispute between TR and these "maudlin fanatics" was on the justice of taking Indian lands. For the young historian who posited the "displacement" of weak races by the strong, the matter seemed very clear. Roosevelt wrote that "it was wholly impossible to avoid conflicts with the weaker race," adding that much "maudlin nonsense" had been written about the Indian removal by people like Jackson and Manypenny.[25] "The simple truth is," Roosevelt stated in an old and standard argument which rarely changed, "that they [the Indians] had no possible title to most of the lands we took, not that of occupancy, and at the most were in possession merely by having butchered the previous inhabitants."[26]

24. TR, *Thomas Hart Benton*, in *Works*, VIII, 45.
25. TR, *The Winning of the West*, in *Works*, X, 90–94.
26. TR, *Thomas Hart Benton*, in *Works*, VIII, 44.

Whereas many Americans had for a long time casually adduced the Indian's lack of legal title as evidence justifying dispossession, Roosevelt employed the argument with great fervor. He argued that "to recognize the Indian ownership of the limitless prairies and forests of this continent—that is to consider the dozen squalid savages who hunted at long intervals over a territory of a thousand square miles as owning it outright—necessarily implies a similar recognition of the claims of every white hunter, squatter, horse thief or wandering cattleman."[27] Moreover, in a fit of intellectual overkill he proclaimed that the nation's Indian policy must not be blamed for the violence which was its hallmark but for the "weakness it displayed, because of its short-sightedness, and its occasional leaning to the policy of the sentimental humanitarians."

Although almost all the active battlefield conflict between Indians and whites had ended by the time Roosevelt began to take an active hand in national political life, he did play a role as Civil Service commissioner and president in implementing and developing policies concerning Indians and dealt with a few such matters while governor of New York. Most of his statements concerning Indians were based upon ideas he had formulated as early as the 1880s when he returned from Dakota and set to work on *The Winning of the West*. "Nowadays," he wrote in 1889, "we undoubtedly ought to break up the great Indian reservations, disregard the tribal governments, allot the land in severalty (with, however, only a limited power of alienation), and treat the Indians as we do other citizens, with certain exceptions, for their sakes as well as ours."[28] Besides allocating lands to individual Indians (and thus furthering the destruction of their tribal culture) Roosevelt also "warmly" favored employing Indians in agency work. "I should take the civilized members of the different tribes and put them to work in instructing their fellows in farming, blacksmithing, and the like, and should extend the present system of paid Indian judges and police," he told Joseph G. Thorp in 1891.[29]

27. TR, *The Winning of the West*, in *Works*, X, 91.
28. *Ibid.*, 92.
29. TR to Joseph Gilbert Thorp, Jr., February 9, 1891, in *Letters*, I, 238.

Despite his harsh estimates of Indians and his adherence to conventional approaches to dealing with the "Indian problem," Roosevelt occasionally made decisions during his six-year tenure as a member of the United States Civil Service Commission which suggested that his instincts for reform could overpower his denigration of Indians and Indian character. Throughout this period, he worked closely with Herbert Welsh, one of the founders of the Indian Rights Association, in a series of attempts at reforming administration of Indian affairs. Roosevelt cooperated with Welsh in seeing that white murderers of Indians were hunted down and in opposing corrupt or unqualified candidates for positions in the Indian Service under Civil Service regulations. Welsh, whose background and reformist tendencies were similar to Roosevelt's, valued the efforts of the Civil Service commissioner in behalf of the Indian Rights Association and urged that Roosevelt be named to head the Indian Service. Still, he often encountered a cautious Roosevelt who wrote strong statements condemning outrages against Indians but refused to have the condemnations made public. Nevertheless, it appears that Welsh believed that Roosevelt had rendered valuable service to the Indian Rights Associations and to the efforts to regulate the corruption-ridden Indian Service.[30]

Roosevelt's contacts with Indians and his interests in Indian policy waned during his terms as police commissioner of New York and assistant secretary of the navy, but when he began to assemble his regiment of Rough Riders months in advance of the outbreak of the Spanish-American War, he included a number of individuals of Indian extraction whom he admired for their abilities as fighters. After the war he showered praise upon these men whose forefathers he had found so reprehensible. His contact with Indians was minimal during his governorship of New York from 1899 until 1901, but he did name a commission charged with looking into the affairs of New York Indians in 1900. Later the same year in accepting the Republican vice-

30. William T. Hagan, "Civil Service Commissioner Theodore Roosevelt and the Indian Rights Association," *Pacific Historical Review*, XLIV (1975), 187–200.

presidential nomination he made a lengthy statement on Indian policy which reflected his basic assumptions that Indians who had survived the encounter with the white man should be gradually incorporated into American society. Some "communities" of Indians, Roosevelt noted, had already reached a level entitling them to "stand on an absolute equality with all our citizens of white blood." [31]

As president, Roosevelt repeated the general theme that Indians could gradually be fitted for membership in white society, but the initiation requirements seemed rather high in spite of the assimilation rhetoric. In his first Annual Message to the Congress in 1901, he stressed that the time had come to ignore tribes and "to recognize the Indian as an individual" who should be treated "like the white man." But the treatment TR prescribed for Indians varied greatly from the norm for whites. Education should be elementary and largely industrial. "The need for higher education among the Indians," he added, is "very, very limited." Moreover, Roosevelt argued that by reducing the amount of subsistence to the Indians they would be forced "through sheer necessity to work for a livelihood." Finally, the president observed, "in dealing with the aboriginal races few things are more important than to preserve them from the terrible physical and moral degradation resulting from the liquor traffic." [32]

In accordance with his most basic beliefs about the necessity of assimilation, much of his presidential rhetoric related to the Indians' "ultimate absorption into the body of our people." [33] Roosevelt argued that whites and Indians should marry and interbreed until the Indian had disappeared as a racial type. Although he had always objected strenuously to interra-

31. TR to Philip C. Garrett, May 26, 1900, in *Letters*, II, 1311; TR, draft of statement accepting vice-presidential nomination, dated September 15, 1900, in Roosevelt Collection, Library of Congress.

32. Roosevelt discussed the Indian problem in his first five annual messages as president, omitted Indians in the next two, and gave only fleeting notice in his last message in 1908. See TR, *State Papers as Governor and President*, in *Works*, XVII, 150, 189, 228, 279, 384, and 619.

33. *Ibid.*, XVIII, 189.

cial marriages between whites and Orientals and whites and blacks, he argued that it should become official United States government policy to encourage white-red intermixture. Willingness to countenance intermixture with Indians reflected Roosevelt's staunch belief in the power of the white race to assimilate most other racial types and the equally important conviction that the small number of remaining Indians could hardly threaten white ascendancy. For years he had accepted the idea that white and red marriages were acceptable, remarking in *The Winning of the West* upon the "queer pride which makes a man of English stock unwilling to make a red-skinned woman his wife, though anxious enough to make her his concubine." [34] Although he noted a few years later on a visit to a Sioux reservation in Dakota that "a little race prejudice" existed against "mixed bloods who are part Indian and part white," he believed that the half-breed was superior to the pure Indian, approvingly noting that in Oklahoma mixed blood was often a source of pride. [35] Plenty of evidence existed, Roosevelt argued, to indicate that unions between reds and whites would eventually issue into a white type marked by the best racial and cultural traits of the white race and devoid of the Indian's unlovely traits. Thus, through assimilation the Indian would complete the journey prescribed in Roosevelt's racial theory for inferior races who obstructed the path of white racial destiny: submission, "displacement," and finally loss of identity through racial "assimilation."

During the Roosevelt presidency, Indian policy focused on several key issues, but primarily on the complex questions of management of Indian lands. All through the White House years, TR's decisions in Indian-related matters brought only modest public attention, although some of the "amiable fanatics" and "maudlin sentimentalists" who belonged to the various humanitarian groups supporting Indian rights frequently opposed Roosevelt policies. Land questions often involved reconciling conflicting desires of Indians and whites or disagree-

34. TR, *The Winning of the West*, in *Works*, X, 38.
35. Quoted in Sinkler, *The Racial Attitudes of American Presidents*, 402.

ments between various Indian groups. Throughout most of the
controversies TR adhered to the belief that Indians should be
allotted land in severalty but he had no qualms about "throw-
ing open to actual homemakers for settlement the surplus land
in the Indian reservations."[36]

Roosevelt repeatedly stressed to Secretary of the Interior
Ethan A. Hitchcock and to officials in the Indian Service the
need for fair treatment of the Indians and he gave force to his
words with attempts to purge the Indian Service of embezzlers,
cheats, and influence peddlers.[37] In dealing directly with Indians, however, TR clearly regarded them as "backward people" requiring firm treatment by their white masters. "I wish to
be as much a father to the red people as to the white," Roosevelt told Chief No Shirt of the Umadilla tribe who had come to
Washington to press for redress of grievances. Roosevelt was
"sorry to learn" that the chief "had followed [his] own will like
a headstrong child" instead of working through the regular
channels of the government bureaucracy in presenting his complaints. Most Indian problems, and especially land problems,
could be traced to the Indians themselves, the president informed the chief, and he hoped that in the future No Shirt
would "try to set . . . a good example of upright and industri-
ous life, patience under difficulties, and respect for the authority" of the officers of the Indian Service. "If you try as hard to
help them [the Indian agents] as you do to find something in
their conduct to censure, you will be surprised to discover how
much real satisfaction life holds in store for you," the president
admonished.[38] Not all of Roosevelt's actions during the presidency were so fatherly. In 1908, when a small group of Indians
clashed with troops on an Indian reservation, Roosevelt justified the killing of several of the men on the basis of his racial
theories:

> The stage of development reached by any group of Indians, their
> attitude toward the Government, and the nearness of their con-

36. TR to Elihu Root, June 2, 1904, in *Letters*, IV, 812.
37. TR to Ethan A. Hitchcock, October 10, 1905, *ibid.*, V, 52–53.
38. TR to Chief No Shirt, May 18, 1905, *ibid.*, IV, 1185–88.

tact with civilization, must always be studied before deciding what practice shall be followed in dealing with their offenses. Devoutly as all of us may look forward to the day when the most backward Indian shall have been brought to the point where he can be governed just as the ignorant white man is governed in one of our civilized communities, that day has not arrived. The surest way to delay its coming is to obstruct the efforts of the Government to deal with Indians, who are still, like the outlaw Navajos [those who were killed] in a wild state, in the only manner which will command their respect and thus bring them to a better realization of their obligation to their neighbors.[39]

Despite the strident tone of much of President Roosevelt's rhetoric, the harsh estimates of Indians which had characterized much of his earlier historical scholarship seemed to have softened slightly during the White House years. While the president remained wedded to the ideas which supported the murder of great numbers of Indians and the conquest of their lands, he did attempt to rectify some of the past wrongs of federal Indian policy and encourage a more humanitarian treatment of some Indians. All of this, of course, is at wide variance with the blood-thirsty Roosevelt of the 1880s who reportedly proclaimed: "I don't go so far as to think that the only good Indians are dead Indians, but I believe nine out of every ten are, and I shouldn't like to inquire too closely into the case of the tenth."[40]

The change in Roosevelt's approach to Indian affairs can probably be ascribed to his growing sense of social justice and reform. Moreover, his personal encounters with Indians in the West while Civil Service commissioner had at least exposed him to the gross inequities in the white man's treatment of the American aborigine, and that experience appears to have had an effect. While president, TR had also shown signs of a growing regard for the uniqueness of Indian culture and on several occasions he encouraged both study of Indian society and main-

39. TR to John D. Long *et al.*, December 29, 1908, *ibid.*, VI, 1449; TR to Mrs. Francis Lee, December 29, 1908, *ibid.*, 1450–51.
40. Quoted in Hermann Hagedorn, *Roosevelt in the Badlands* (Boston, 1921), 355.

tenance of unique aspects of Indian life.[41] That such large areas of inconsistency could exist in Roosevelt's mind provides a window on the complexity of the man and his ability to react in seemingly contradictory ways to a single racial group.

Whereas the bulk of TR's rhetoric during the presidential years had continued to stress the ignobility of the Indian, experiences after the presidency seemed to further meliorate his estimate of Indian character. During the last five years of his life, the former president enjoyed several expeditions into the Southwest, where for the first time he observed the living styles of the Navajo and Hopi. He came to admire both cultures and concluded that within these two tribes "ordinary life—not the strange heathen ceremonies—was that of a remarkably advanced, and still advancing semi-civilization; not savagery at all." These observations led him to recommend that a rethinking of some aspects of Indian policy might be justified. If the Navajo and the Hopi were actually drifting toward civilization, it might be well to allow the retention of lands by the tribes rather than allotting them in severalty.[42] And, the government might wish to consider establishing a "half-way house" to ease the transition of Indians into white society. Without this aid, Roosevelt believed, "they may never reach their destination and stand on a level with the white man."[43] Nevertheless, Roosevelt still believed that even these tribes owed their progress "to the presence of the white man in their neighborhood," though he incorporated into his mature philosophy of the Indian the notion that perhaps elements of aboriginal culture were worth preserving.

There is big room for improvement; but so there is among whites; and while the improvement should be along the lines of gradual assimilation to the life of the best whites, it should unquestionably be so shaped as to preserve and develop the very element of native culture possessed by these Indians—which as I have

41. See, for example, TR to Ethan A. Hitchcock, July 22, 1903, in *Letters*, III, 523.
42. TR, "Across the Navajo Desert," in *Works*, IV, 28.
43. *Ibid.*, 39.

already said, if thus preserved and developed, may in the end become an important contribution to American cultural life. Ultimately I hope the Indian will be absorbed into the white population, on a full equality; as was true for instance, of the Indians who served in my own regiment, the Rough Riders; as is true on the Navajo reservation itself of two of the best men thereon, both in government employ, both partly of northern Indian blood, and both indistinguishable from the most upright and efficient of the men of pure white blood.[44]

If Roosevelt minimized his antipathy toward the Indian during the last years of his life, the change did not alter the most basic principles of his racial world view. The late-discovered admiration for Indian culture stands as an adjunct to a theory of race which stressed the red man's savagery and posited his disappearance through displacement and assimilation. For Theodore Roosevelt the Indian would always remain a victim of white racial destiny.

44. TR, "The Hopi Snake-Dance," in *Works*, IV, 53–54.

CHAPTER V

Blacks

Although Theodore Roosevelt considered blacks in world perspective—observing and evaluating American, Latin American, and African blacks on the basis of their racial pedigree and "place" in the civilization-development scheme which he posited—he naturally gave heavy emphasis to the problems and perplexities which the joint presence of large numbers of blacks and whites on the North American continent had created. The "fact" that blacks could not be absorbed into the national bloodstream, coupled with social tradition, historical convictions about the inferiority of blacks, and the belief that blacks were better breeders than white Americans, all led Roosevelt to regard the "Negro problem" as a very special dilemma.

Roosevelt's understanding of the "Negro problem" matured in an age of intensifying racism in the United States. From the close of the Civil War, seven years after his birth, to the end of World War I, a year before he died, the powerful social mores of a racist society combined with repressive "Jim Crow" legislation and reactionary judicial decisions to ensure that blacks would be relegated to positions of social, economic, and political inferiority in American life. With the institutionalization of racism, blacks also found themselves abandoned by the federal government and the Republican party, once regarded hopefully as the best vehicle for full inclusion in American society. Although some Republican politicians sought for a time to keep the great issues of the Civil War alive, the period between the withdrawal of federal troops from the South in 1877 and the beginning of the First World War was one of steady erosion of black rights including the right to vote, the right to serve on juries, and the right to public accommodations. Deprival of civil rights constituted only one phase of the worsening position of blacks in American society, for while the courts and Republican politicians ignored the reimposition of white control in the South, they also turned their backs to the steady growth of grisly racial violence. Mutilations, dismemberments, and lynchings increased frightfully as the nation acquiesced in the notion that white southerners best understood the "Negro problem" and how to cope with it.

The same period also saw the efflorescence of a variety of racial theories which provided a convenient rationale for the political and social debasement of Afro-Americans. The white American mind, long accustomed to thinking of the Negro as inferior, now confronted a formidable range of ideas which propounded a black inferiority based upon "scientific" evidence as well as upon the fables and myths of the popular culture. These clusters of racist notions flowed from the mixture of science, pseudoscience, and racial prejudice which characterized the antiblack beliefs of the slavocracy and found spokesmen in individuals like Josiah Nott, the Alabama physician whose 1855 book *Types of Mankind* distilled the research of several disciplines in an effort to establish the physical and mental inferiority of blacks.

In the post–Civil War era, the pace of antiblack thinking accelerated as Americans drew heavily upon the writings of European writers who were investigating race. Among the most influential was Count Arthur de Gobineau, whose book *The Inequality of Human Races* advanced a theory of the rise and fall of civilizations based on racial considerations and argued that a "strict despotism" described the relationship which should exist between white governors and their black subjects. Numerous other Europeans influenced the growth of anti-Negro thought in the United States and included thinkers like Sir Francis Galton, who emphasized the importance of heredity in describing the Negro as "childish, stupid, and simpleton like"; the Frenchman Gustave LeBon, who argued for inherent racial psychologies; and the German biologist August Weis-

mann, who promoted a brand of hereditarian determinism. Still
others borrowed from the French physical anthropologists in
correlating physical traits of blacks with racial inferiority, while
some American racists wrenched arguments for black inferiority from the theories of Charles Darwin.

In America, the multitude of interpreters of antiblack thought
wove their ideas into virtually every area of scholarly inquiry
and public policy. Although nearly all of the American thinkers wrote in a white supremacist vein, they differed in the intensity of their antipathy toward blacks and in the character of
the "solutions" which they proposed for the "problem." Still,
they shared certain assumptions about black inferiority and
race relations which suggested the universality of antiblack
feeling in TR's America.

White Americans assumed that blacks differed so significantly from whites in physical appearance, temperament, and
intellectual capacity that only the slow process of evolution
might eventually bring the two races closer together. In this
framework, miscegenation between whites and blacks could not
be tolerated because it was believed to result in a debasement
of the white stock and would prove retrogressive to "white civilization." Similarly, racial prejudice on the part of whites seemed
perfectly natural at a time when blacks aspired to equality with
whites and were no longer subject to the constant supervision
of slavery. From these propositions, nearly all Americans de-
duced that the future of blacks in the United States could not
measurably improve and that Afro-Americans should either be
removed from the population or forced to conform to a caste
system.[1]

Roosevelt's frequent invocation of the idea of equal opportunity for all Americans regardless of race and his occasional efforts in behalf of blacks earned him a reputation among both
his contemporaries and among many historians as a racial

1. The best discussion of antiblack thought in America during Roosevelt's lifetime is Idus A. Newby's *Jim Crow's Defense: Anti-Negro Thought in America, 1900–
1930*. The above paragraphs are based primarily on Newby, 1–16; quotations taken
from 9, 11.

"moderate." Certainly Roosevelt the race thinker should not be portrayed in the same terms as such hucksters of anti-Negro mythology as Madison Grant or Charles Carroll; nor does he belong in the same category as racist politicians of the ilk of "Pitchfork" Ben Tillman, James K. Vardaman, or Tom Watson. More properly, Roosevelt is associated with the group of theorists who promoted the vision of racial equipotentiality and with those politicians who publicly deplored the oppression of American blacks yet opposed "social equality." Thus, although Roosevelt may have been a moderating force in an age of high racism, he nevertheless harbored strong feelings about the inferiority of blacks, feelings which suggest the pervasiveness of racism and the harsh character of racial "moderation" in turn-of-the-century America.

In order to fasten more firmly upon the "place" of blacks in American society, TR developed an explanatory scheme for the contradiction between American democratic ideology and the reality of a caste society based upon race. In Roosevelt's system blacks as a youthful race stood much closer to savagery than to civilization in the evolutionary scale. While they could progress individually and as a race the pace of improvement could be extremely slow, perhaps just as slow as the evolutionary process itself. If democratic beliefs compelled him to argue that blacks should be received into American political society, he insisted on the need for a very gradual entry without "social equality." As a believer in Lamarckianism he had little difficulty justifying such repressive "gradualism" in the faith that blacks like other races would acquire the characteristics necessary for their ascension to the evolutionary heights. While this Lamarckian emphasis on the equipotentiality of blacks underscored Roosevelt's belief that blacks were human beings and not a subspecies as many theorists argued, it also exposed his reliance upon the doctrine of acquired characteristics as an intellectual justification for a limited theoretical assimilation of blacks into American society.

Blacks figured in many of the important phases and events

of Roosevelt's life. As a youth he reveled in the stories of black life on the ancestral plantation in Georgia, the home of his mother's family the Bullochs, and as a young historian he examined, however minimally, the black experience in American history—or more accurately the instances of black history which seemed to impinge on the flow of white American history. In addition, Roosevelt had to confront blacks in all aspects of his military and political career. From his days as an ambitious young state legislator seeking national attention in the 1880s through his tenure as Civil Service commissioner, Spanish-American War colonel, governor of New York, vice-president, and finally as president of the United States, he called for a turn-of-the-century version of "equal" treatment for all Americans regardless of race. And in the years after leaving the White House he indulged in a variety of activities which emphasized his lifelong fascination with blackness and the subject of race, observing the behavior of African tribesmen, recording in the manner of a cultural anthropologist the life-style of Latin-American blacks, and offering opinions about the course of black life around the world.

Roosevelt's images of blacks in history were shaped by his childhood encounter with the southern heritage bequeathed him by his mother, an "unreconstructed rebel" who told young Theodore countless stories about life in antebellum Georgia.[2] Roosevelt always fondly recalled those anecdotes in later life, remembering with special relish the roles of his two uncles in the Confederate naval service who departed for what must have seemed a heroic English exile after the war. In his autobiography Roosevelt described the southern heritage of his family proudly, in a manner which at once revealed his conception of antebellum southern life and his fondness for romanticizing the institution of slavery. Although he did not visit the ancestral home at Roswell until after he became president, Roosevelt felt as if he knew "every nook and corner" of the

2. Theodore Roosevelt to Hugo Münsterberg, February 8, 1916, in *Letters*, VIII, 1017.

place. His mother's recollections had included many stories about the Bulloch slaves including a "fascinating" tale about "a very old darky called Bear Bob" and anecdotes of "Mom' Grace, who was for a time my mother's nurse, and whom I had supposed to be dead, but who greeted me when I did come to Roswell, very respectable, and apparently with years of life before her." The two "chief personages," however, in the tales of blacks told to Roosevelt were "Daddy Luke, the negro overseer, and his wife Mom' Charlotte." According to TR, Daddy Luke and Mom' Charlotte had "resolutely refused to be emancipated or leave the place" after the Civil War. In a comment reminiscent of the hoariest of southern apologetics for slavery, he announced that he had "inherited the care of them when [his] mother died";[3] a few years earlier he had commented privately that he was "yet supporting one or two venerable black imposters who were slaves in the family before the war." There was a "good side to slavery," Roosevelt argued, but he also added that he knew "what a hideous side there was to it, and this was the important side."[4]

If Roosevelt's filiopietistic instincts toward his southern heritage ran strong, a counter current of hostility toward slavery and other southern institutions also flowed through his mind. While he denounced slavery on moral and political grounds, his denunciation was freighted with a racial self-centeredness common among turn-of-the-century white intellectuals. Evidence of the intellectual position which this tension bred in his mind appears in his early literary endeavors.

Although Roosevelt in his first serious literary efforts of the 1880s and 1890s criticized the immorality of slavery, he gave greater stress to its adverse effects on the historical development of white America. In the opening chapter of *The Winning of the West* the young scholar betrayed a certain moral obtuseness as he bewailed the appearance of slavery in North America as "a crime whose short-sighted folly was worse than its

3. TR, *Autobiography*, in *Works*, XXII, 7.
4. TR to George F. R. Henderson, February 14, 1899, in *Letters*, II, 945.

guilt."[5] Slavery, said Roosevelt, "must of necessity exercise the most baleful influence upon any slaveholding people, and especially upon those members of the dominant caste who do not themselves own slaves." He continued: "Moreover, the Negro, unlike so many of the inferior races, does not dwindle away in the presence of the white man. He holds his own; indeed under the conditions of American slavery he increased faster than the white, threatening to supplant him." Blacks had actually "supplanted" whites in "certain of the West Indian Islands," the young historian reminded his readers. Thus, the "sin of the white in enslaving the black has been visited upon the head of the wrong-doer by his victim with a dramatically terrible completeness of revenge." Roosevelt believed that blacks might have "supplanted" American whites if slavery had not been abolished and the rate of increase among blacks thus diminished. While enforced servitude was "ethically abhorrent to all rightminded men" and should be "condemned without stint on this ground alone," TR clearly perceived its abolition as being most valuable for averting a threatened black inundation of white America. The American "master caste" had had most to fear from slavery and the future president argued that upper-class whites should have condemned slavery "even more strongly, because it invariably in the end threatens [their] existence." He concluded that the "presence of the negro is the real problem." Slavery had been "merely the worst possible method of solving the problem." Before abolition, problem and solution had been one. Now, Roosevelt wrote, though differences of opinion existed with regard to solving the "problem," no one would disagree that "the worst foes, not only of humanity and civilization, but especially of the white race in America, were those white men who brought slaves from Africa, and who fostered the spread of slavery in the States and Territories of the American Republic."[6]

Thus, Roosevelt, like many of his contemporaries, subordi-

5. TR, *The Winning of the West*, in *Works*, X, 9.
6. *Ibid.*, XI, 260–61.

nated the moral depravity of slavery to a view of the institution which stressed its harm to "white civilization" and the "master caste," hardly a position consistent with his repeated private and public condemnations of slaveholders and slavery but one which offers a revealing glimpse into the racial self-centeredness of Theodore Roosevelt and his time.

From Roosevelt's point of view, slavery had been less a problem than was the central problem posed by the presence of blacks in white America. While he may have wished that blacks could be removed from the American political scene, throughout his political career he accepted the idea that they were to remain permanently in the United States. The issue then became to define their position in American society, and in his attempts to do so Roosevelt focused on the question of how much black participation in political life seemed desirable. Although his response to this matter often varied with changing political circumstances, two principal questions were reckoned with in this consideration; first, should blacks vote, and second, on what basis might a black person attain political office.

Roosevelt's first public attempt to deal with the issue of black participation in the American electoral process occurred at the Republican National Convention in Chicago in 1884. There the twenty-six-year-old politician vigorously endorsed the nomination of John R. Lynch of Mississippi for temporary chairman. The Lynch nomination grew out of a feud between the convention supporters of James G. Blaine and dissident forces headed by Roosevelt and Henry Cabot Lodge. After an all-night session in a hotel room, it was decided to nominate Lynch, although some of Roosevelt's and Lodge's allies feared the effects of nominating a black. Lodge made the nomination speech and Roosevelt seconded it, arguing that individual delegates should be held accountable for their votes on the matter. He invoked Lincoln's memory as one who "broke the fetters of the slave and rent them asunder" and concluded that it was a "fitting thing for us to choose to preside over this convention one of that race whose right to sit within these walls is due to the blood and the treasure so lavishly spent by the founders of the Republican Party."[7]

At this youthful stage of his political career, Roosevelt's opinions about the extent of participation of any race in American politics rested primarily upon his conviction that centuries of evolutionary development preceded attainment of the level requisite for participation in affairs of state. While he argued for the largely symbolic election of a black to the position of temporary chairman, he harbored no conviction that the mass of blacks were ready for active involvement in political matters, constitutional amendments notwithstanding. Even the "white" races had had to pass through developmental stages before they became fit for self-government. The English race, for example, at the time of Cromwell, "were not fit yet to govern themselves unaided." "Such fitness," Roosevelt explained in Lamarckian terms, "is not a God-given natural right, but comes to a race only through the slow growth of centuries, and then only to those races which possess an immense reserve fund of strength, common sense, and morality."[8] For blacks, self-government would be a "slowly learned and difficult art which our people have taught themselves by the labor of a thousand years." Such a skill could not be "grasped in a day by a people only just emerging from conditions of life which our ancestors left behind them in the dim years before history dawned."[9]

Roosevelt's insistence upon the election of Lynch presaged his later ideas and actions with respect to black political participation. Even though he believed that a few blacks had acquired through the evolutionary process the necessary characteristics for participation in politics, for Roosevelt the mass of blacks remained in ignorance and backwardness and would have to wait until the interacting forces of racial inheritance and environment prepared them to assume more responsible

7. TR, "The Nomination for Temporary Chairman of the Republican Convention," in *Works*, XVI, 69–70.

8. TR, *Oliver Cromwell*, in *Works*, XIII, 358–59.

9. TR, Speech at Arlington, Virginia, May 30, 1903, in Roosevelt Collection, Library of Congress.

roles. This dichotomy of 1884 persisted until the end. Roosevelt's overall view of blacks was thus bifurcated into something
approximating a class division. The privileged were to participate in American life while the masses had to wait patiently
until notified of their eligibility.

Occasionally, however, young Roosevelt criticized southern
efforts to prevent blacks from voting. During an 1885 speaking
tour, while characteristically disclaiming any attempt to "in-
veigh against Southerners for what is now the fashion to call
their ancient history," he denounced attempts to suppress the
black Republican vote, complained that "naturally Republican" states like South Carolina, Mississippi, and Louisiana
were being "kept solidly Democratic by force and fraud," and
condemned the attempts of New South spokesmen to justify
exclusion of blacks. Roosevelt believed that the New South arguments could be expressed in three principal propositions.
"First, the Negroes are not fit to exercise political rights. Second, they do not want them. Third, and most important, if they
do not want them, they shall not have them." Blacks *did* want
to vote, Roosevelt argued, and Republicans had a responsibility to see that attempts to restrict the suffrage were stopped.
Instead of denouncing the first proposition, however, he only
labeled it an assertion which could not be "advanced in good
faith as a reason for fraudulently disfranchising a class of our
fellow citizens by any man who honestly believes in our American theory of government." In an era when the Republican
party gradually abdicated its responsibility to blacks, Roosevelt would only go so far as to call for the force of public opinion to be brought to bear against disfranchisement and to note
that "under the heroic leadership of men like George W. Cable
there had already sprung up in the South a small but apprecia-
ble and growing sentiment against it." [10]

The issue of black office holding first arose for Roosevelt
when he became Civil Service commissioner in 1889. In matters concerning appointments he consistently claimed to adhere to the policy of appointing the best men without regard

10. TR, "The Campaign of 1885," in *Works*, XVI, 105–107.

for race, color, or religion. Writing to Hugh McKittrick in 1895, Commissioner Roosevelt explained, "We stated explicitly in our report upon the the Bureau of Engraving and Printing" that while "the law contained no provision which enabled us to guarantee equal treatment to black and white . . . the spirit of the law undoubtedly meant that there should be this equal treatment." When blacks encountered discrimination, he continued, "we intended to make public the facts, so that we might at least excite the indignation of honest men about them." Roosevelt did not refer to all blacks of course, only to those who met his standards and whom he felt were sufficiently advanced to merit governmental posts.[11]

As governor of New York, Roosevelt maintained the same posture. He advised the Utica, New York, chief of police that "if a colored man could be put on your force it would be a very good thing," and on another occasion he wrote a state official that Charles W. Anderson, "a really good Colored Republican leader of this state," desired that a few blacks be appointed to state offices. Roosevelt told the official that if he could "get the right type of man, this would be a good thing to do."[12] Later, accused by a black leader of appointing an insufficient number of blacks to positions in government, the governor defensively replied that it was well known that he only had a "very limited" number of appointments and needed "men of peculiar stamp." He observed that he had appointed a black man, Gaius Bolin, to the Pan American Exposition Board in "a position of high trust and honor." "Relative to their numbers," Governor Roosevelt argued, "the colored men have received due justice."[13] To T. Thomas Fortune, black editor and politician, Roosevelt complained that blacks themselves were to blame for the limited number of appointments: "The trouble lies in the rancorous factional feeling among the colored men themselves." In particular, he added, the problem arose with regard to "large" ap-

11. TR to Hugh McKittrick, February 21, 1895, in *Letters*, I, 427.
12. TR to John Williams, April 12, 1899 and TR to James M. Varnum, February 21, 1899, both in Roosevelt Collection, Library of Congress.
13. TR to P. Butler Thompkins, July 5, 1899, in Roosevelt Collection, Library of Congress.

pointments. He had successfully secured for blacks a "number of small appointments" but when he sought to appoint Fortune himself to a high position he had been "met with a perfect chorus of opposition [from blacks], and so with every colored man whom he deemed of prominence." This state of affairs, Roosevelt added, "seems to me to be very unfortunate."[14]

However uncomfortable such situations made him, Roosevelt continued during the 1890s to profess basic belief in racial equipotentiality, but he always made it clear that the distance from the black racial position to the status of the superior races remained great and that blacks had only begun to traverse it. An example of Governor Roosevelt's estimate of the continued low station of blacks in his overall scheme of racial development occurred in his evaluation of black soldiers who served with him in Cuba. In a series of articles in *Scribner's Magazine*, Roosevelt stressed that "colored" regulars had generally fought well but that differences existed between white and black troops which should be weighed in any decision to use black soldiers on a long-term basis. Blacks were "particularly dependent" upon white officers, lacked the capacity to lead, and had submitted to "extraordinary panic" under fire while whites had acted coolly. Principally, however, he charged that black soldiers had fled the front lines during battle, seeking safety in the rear. Only a personal warning and a threat to shoot those involved prevented wholesale mutiny. "Here again," Roosevelt reported, "I attributed the trouble to the superstition and fear of the darkey, natural in those but one generation removed from slavery and but a few generations removed from the wildest savagery."[15]

A lively discussion soon developed over Roosevelt's disparaging remarks when a black federal employee challenged the Rough Rider's account of the incident and found support among both black and white veterans. Blacks had not fled the

14. TR to T. Thomas Fortune, March 27, 1899, in Roosevelt Collection, Library of Congress.
15. TR, *The Rough Riders*, in *Works*, XIII, 109–110; TR to Robert J. Fleming, May 21, 1900, in *Letters*, II, 1305.

lines, it was argued, but had been working with white soldiers to transport wounded troops to the rear areas. According to these witnesses, Roosevelt had erroneously concluded that the blacks were leaving their posts and then threatened to shoot them. Blacks also pointed out that one of TR's fellow officers had severely criticized him on the spot for his battlefield impulsiveness. These witnesses concluded that a chastened Roosevelt had then acknowledged his error in a conversation with the officer.

When Roosevelt's published account of the incident threatened a loss of black votes for the Republican national ticket in 1900, he quickly put forward a revised version of the incident blaming a white captain for ordering the soldiers to the rear. Roosevelt, now the vice-presidential nominee of his party, told the electorate that he would be the "last man in the world to say anything against the colored soldiers."[16] In spite of this disavowal of malice toward the blacks, it is clear that Roosevelt interpreted the Cuban occurrences in a way that conformed to his own beliefs about the level of military skill possessed by blacks and the lengthy period of time required for a race to acquire such skills. For at least five years, he had believed that black military prowess could not approach that of whites for thousands of years. Political considerations forced him to revise his public account of the matter, but there is no evidence to suggest that he changed his privately held views.

Roosevelt renewed his belief in gradual black improvability on the eve of assuming the vice-presidency. In a letter to William H. Lewis, black attorney and later a Roosevelt-appointed assistant United States attorney for New England, he stated what would become a familiar rationale for appointment of blacks and an equally familiar excuse for nonappointment. "My own belief," Roosevelt told Lewis, "has been that the only thing to do is try each man, white or dusky, personally on his own merits, not to lie to scrutinize him, but to do him justice." Some blacks, however, just would not do. Roosevelt told Lewis that

16. James Haney, "Theodore Roosevelt and Afro-Americans, 1901–1912" (Ph.D. dissertation, Kent State University, 1971), 8–12.

he had "gotten in several scrapes" by failing to appoint blacks "who are public talkers, who are great agitators," and while merit would be rewarded, blacks should remember that "the path of the race upward will necessarily be painful." In something of an obiter dictum, he noted that whites were "bound to help the race in every way on the upward path," and that some would lend active support. He concluded with the wish that he could meet Lewis, Paul Dunbar, and Booker Washington to "talk the matter over at length." [17]

In 1901, with the assassination of William McKinley, Roosevelt became president and soon turned his attention to the assortment of complex questions of policy involving black Americans. The nearly eight years of his presidency coincided with one of the most violent periods of antiblack activity in American history as lynchings reached an all-time high, southern legislatures completed the legalized exclusion of blacks from meaningful participation in American life, and racial pogroms occurred with alarming frequency. During this period Roosevelt felt intense political pressures from white southerners to continue the national government's acquiescence in the oppression, but he also had to cope with the expectations of black leaders who hoped for better things from the aristocratic New York Republican who had long preached the need for equality of opportunity.

President Roosevelt typically sought to steer a middle course, with a limited number of federal appointments which he hoped would satisfy black leaders and with simultaneous reassurances to southerners that white appointments greatly exceeded black. Controversies inevitably arose which involved TR's promises to blacks and his reassurances to whites. Two of these, the Indianola, Mississippi, post office affair and the so-called "Crum incident" offer instructive examples of the interplay between Roosevelt's racial theory, political considerations, and personal convictions.

Mrs. Minnie M. Cox had been postmaster at Indianola, Mississippi, for years. First appointed by President Benjamin Har-

---

17. TR to William Henry Lewis, July 26, 1900, in *Letters*, II, 1364–65.

rison when no white Republicans qualified, then reappointed by William McKinley after the Democratic administration of Grover Cleveland, she was a sophisticated, college-educated woman, who quietly conducted the affairs of her office in a manner which suggested that she understood the social mores of white Mississippians. Until a white politician began to covet her position, Mrs. Cox's term had been relatively quiet. Predictably, the local community supported the claim of the white man to the office and began to harass and threaten Mrs. Cox, who ultimately resigned her post.

Roosevelt, whose reforming zeal and concern for his election chances in 1904 had moved him to upgrade the quality of federal appointments, refused to accept Mrs. Cox's resignation and closed the Indianola post office until the postmaster felt she could resume her duties. Throughout the controversy which ensued, Roosevelt stood by Mrs. Cox, who had become a focal point for the racist diatribes of Mississippi politician James K. Vardaman. Only when Mrs. Cox and other black leaders determined that it would be impossible for a black official to serve in the hostile environment of Indianola did Roosevelt appoint a white and reopen the post office.

Contemporaries charged that Roosevelt had acted to curry favor with black Republicans in both the South and North and to strengthen his chances for the party's presidential nomination in 1904, but recent scholarship suggests that the president acted in a way which he believed would show other black officeholders in the South that he would support them as he had Mrs. Cox.[18] However that may be, it is clear that Roosevelt's defense of Mrs. Cox was made easier by his categorization of her as one of the few blacks who had moved ahead of the masses and thus deserved support. From the Indianola affair it is also clear that political considerations did not always alter Roosevelt's racial beliefs and that on occasion he did act in accordance with principles congruent with the theory of equipotentiality.

The so-called Crum incident illustrates another way in which

18. Willard B. Gatewood, *Theodore Roosevelt and the Art of Controversy: Episodes of the White House Years* (Baton Rouge, 1970), 62–89.

Roosevelt reconciled his professions of equality under the law with his racial theories. In this affair, which dragged on for over six years of TR's administration, the president's motives seemed more political, more calculated from the outset to enhance his standing with black Republicans in South Carolina and in the North.

William Crum, a Charleston physician, was one of the "good" Negroes who, in Roosevelt's view, could aspire to positions of responsibility and prominence in American society. Roosevelt decided to appoint Dr. Crum to head the customshouse in Charleston, South Carolina, only after a lengthy period of in-decision and political maneuvering. In making the appoint-ment, the president hoped to allay factional strife within the South Carolina Republican party, neutralize opposition among dissident Republicans, and thus ensure nomination in the Re-publican national convention of 1904. Although it was a posi-tion of indifferent importance (a fact which TR recognized), it nevertheless threw the white supremacists of South Carolina into a frenzy of opposition. Roosevelt supported Crum in the lengthy and vociferous dispute which ensued and realized the desired political results. [Indeed Roosevelt's actions did not disclose any commitment to improving the lot of the great mass of blacks but revealed him once more as willing to take an un-popular stand when the opposition challenged his authority as president.] More important, it showed him once again acting upon his belief that a few, privileged blacks deserved the sup-port of the president of the United States. As Willard Gatewood has concluded, "From the standpoint of practical politics, the appointment could scarcely have been more successful," but it would be erroneous to suggest that TR's administration had developed a policy intended to promote the cause of black civil rights.[19] Thus, the incident stands as another example of Roose-velt's commitment to the advancement of individual blacks when political advantage coincided with ideology.

Aside from these two widely discussed incidents, numerous other conflicts arose concerning the president's appointments

19. *Ibid.*, 133–34.

policies. Roosevelt's frequent and vociferous claims that he had followed a progressive policy with regard to patronage for blacks did not, however, entirely mask the fact that the number of black appointments declined during the 1901–1909 period. Still, Roosevelt continued to insist that he would appoint those blacks to federal positions who raised themselves through personal tenacity and evolutionary process to a level worthy of consideration for appointments. Thus, he could feel comfortably consistent with evolutionary ideology and the rhetoric of equipotentiality alongside Republican politics in that he allowed for the progress of individuals to the level of white men even if the race as a whole remained backward.

In the process of converting rhetoric to principles and proclaiming them as uncompromisable elements of his own moral code, Roosevelt sometimes had to exempt his own presidential acts. Soon after entering the presidency in 1901, he had invited Booker T. Washington to dine with him at the White House, but when a storm of protest from white southerners arose, TR permitted varying accounts of the incident to circulate and by refusing to clarify the issue sought to minimize the strident opposition from southerners while still reaping the benefits of having a "liberal" racial image. Later on, he admitted to friends that the invitation had been a mistake, but in the wake of the dinner he wrote Reconstruction politician and novelist Albion Tourgée and justified his racial ideas in terms of morality. The new president confessed that he had been unable "to think out any solution of the terrible problem offered by the presence of the negro on this continent," but since blacks resided in North America and since they "could neither be killed or driven away" the "wise and honorable and Christian thing to do is to treat each black man and each white man on his merits as a man, giving him no more and no less than he shows himself worthy to have." While he did not intend to "offend the prejudices of anyone else," he declared that he would not permit those prejudices to impinge upon his principles.[20]

20. In this letter Roosevelt told Tourgée that he had "felt a moment's qualm on inviting him [Washington] because of his color," that this had made him feel ashamed and had made him "hasten to send the invitation." TR to Albion Winegar Tourgée,

Despite Roosevelt's doubts about the wisdom of black political participation and about the prudence of Reconstruction leaders in adopting the Fifteenth Amendment, he neither advocated nor endorsed disfranchisement.[21] Once he had accepted the theoretical necessity of preserving the franchise for blacks he scolded acquaintances who favored explicit and open disfranchisement policies. In a lengthy letter to his old friend and Harvard classmate Owen Wister, the president reproved the author of *The Virginian* for justifying southern efforts to curtail black voting. Roosevelt gently criticized Wister's latest book, *Lady Baltimore*, which reflected most racial stereotypes held by nineteenth-century South Carolina aristocrats.[22] While the objects of Roosevelt's criticism were harsh southern racial attitudes and by implication the views of Wister himself, the president revealed his own low estimate of most blacks. "Now as to the negroes!" Roosevelt wrote, "I entirely agree with you that as a race and in the mass they are altogether inferior to the whites." Yet in an effort to qualify this sweeping condemnation, he went on to remark that "admitting all that can truthfully be said against the Negro, it also remains true that a great deal that is untrue is said against him; and that much more is untruthfully said in favor of the white man who lives beside and upon him." In a characteristic hedge he coupled with the admission that blacks were "generally" unfit to vote some criticism of Wister's apologia for southern repression and a strong dismissal of the idea that blacks had "become worse" since the Civil War as "the veriest nonsense." Freedmen, the Lamarckian Roosevelt admonished Wister, had "on the whole become better."

November 8, 1901, in *Letters*, III, 190–91. The most cogent interpretation of the Booker T. Washington affair is Willard Gatewood's essay "The Roosevelt-Washington Dinner: The Accretion of Folklore," in Gatewood, *Theodore Roosevelt and the Art of Controversy*, 32–61.

21. TR to Henry Cabot Lodge, December 4, 1916, *ibid.*, VIII, 1132.

22. *Lady Baltimore* was an extremely popular novel which remained at the top of the best-seller list for a number of weeks. For a discussion of Wister's relationship with Roosevelt, see Owen Wister, *Roosevelt: The Story of a Friendship* (New York, 1930).

Although Roosevelt charged Wister with presenting an unfair view of the capabilities and character of blacks, he confessed that his presidential efforts to deal effectively with racial problems had been largely unsuccessful. He claimed some success for efforts to minimize the spread of peonage, but sadly admitted that white southerners had often successfully obstructed many of his attempts to help blacks. When he consulted southern opinion in formulating policy, the results turned out "worse than in any other way." The Charlestonians whom Wister warmly depicted in his novel particularly offended Roosevelt's carefully nurtured sense of individualism and he bitterly denounced them for the enforced consensus under which they lived: "I know of no people in the North so slavishly conventional, so slavishly afraid of expressing any opinion hostile to or different from that held by their neighbors as is true of the Southerners, and most especially of the Charleston aristocrats, on all vital questions."

Southern sexual exploitation of blacks especially aroused the puritanical Roosevelt, who as self-appointed spokesman for national virtue abhorred the code of behavior which allowed southern whites to "keep" black women and to sire their children. "They shriek in public about miscegenation," he confided to Wister, "but they leer as they talk to me privately of the colored mistresses and colored children of white men whom they know." Moreover, he complained, southern politicians "who in the Senate yell about the purity of the white blood, deceived me into appointing postmasters whom I found had colored mistresses and colored children."[23]

Throughout his seven years in the White House Roosevelt often repeated such assertions and seemed especially to enjoy tweaking the sensibilities of white southerners, particularly those who opposed him politically. When Robert Goodwyn Rhett of Charleston wrote to complain of the impending appointment of Dr. Crum, Roosevelt's hortatory reply could have been aimed at one of Wister's aristocrats whom he so thor-

23. TR to Owen Wister, July 27, 1906, in *Letters*, V, 226–28.

oughly despised. If Rhett could provide evidence of Crum's unfitness the president would listen, but he cautioned the South Carolinian that color alone would not bar Crum from office. Although he promised to listen to the "likes and dislikes of the people of each locality," doors would not be shut to men on the basis of color. The matter of "negro domination" did not enter into it at all, the president related, as he correctly pointed out that the "enormous majority" of his appointments had been white—and that those appointments had also been made on the basis of character alone. "It seems to me," Roosevelt counseled Rhett, "that it is a good thing from every standpoint to let the colored man know that if he shows in marked degree the qualities of good citizenship—the qualities which in a white man we feel are entitled to reward—then he himself will not be cut off from all hope of similar reward."[24] When another Charlestonian declared that South Carolinians would never submit to "the rule of the African" and that the appointment constituted an affront to "white blood," Roosevelt curtly repeated the argument he made to Rhett and added that he could really not understand why anyone would think that he would refuse to appoint an individual because of color. Moreover, he expressed at least some doubt about the writer's assertion that blacks as a whole were yet unfit to assume public positions: "If, as you hold, the great bulk of the colored people are not yet fit in point of character and influence to hold such positions, it seems to me that it is worth while [*sic*] putting a premium upon the effort among them to achieve the character standing which will fit them."[25]

Although Roosevelt's willingness to support black interests declined during his second term, he continued to use the old rhetoric and to make the effort to placate both blacks and southern whites.[26] He reassured Clark Howell of the Atlanta *Constitution* in terms reminiscent of the letter to Rhett that his appointments policy had nothing to do with "social equality" and

24. TR to Robert Goodwyn Rhett, November 10, 1902, *ibid.*, III, 375–76.
25. TR to James Adger Smith, November 26, 1902, *ibid.*, III, 383–85.
26. See Haney, "Theodore Roosevelt and Afro-Americans, 1901–1912."

"negro domination" and that to connect them with such remote questions would be as absurd as relating them to "the
nebular hypothesis or the theory of atoms." [27]

Throughout his presidency the preponderance of his public
and private pronouncements had suggested that he intended
to hold to a philosophy of exclusion bolstered by his belief that
the black was largely incapable of assuming the role of citizen.[28] After the presidential years, Roosevelt's convictions that
blacks had not acquired the necessary characteristics for political participation grew even stronger. By 1912, perplexed
with his earlier inability to deal with the great number of black-
related problems and willing to sacrifice principle for political
gain, he prepared to exclude blacks altogether from represen-
tation in the Progressive party convention with the argument
that it was in their best interest. In 1916 he confided in Henry
Cabot Lodge his belief that the "great majority of the negroes
in the South are wholly unfit for the suffrage." Extending the
vote to these blacks could "reduce parts of the South to the
level of Haiti." [29] Thus, although much of his public rhetoric
suggested otherwise, Roosevelt remained convinced that blacks
would become full citizens only very slowly. In the meantime,
full citizenship would go only to those "good," privileged blacks
like Booker T. Washington, William Crum, and Minnie Cox.[30]

Whereas Roosevelt continued to profess equal opportunity
for qualified blacks, the larger structure within which he accounted for his view of black political roles contained a set of
interrelated ideas which embodied his expectations for black
behavior in general and provided a formula for social control
of nonwhites by whites. Blacks were for Roosevelt a "back-

27. TR to Clark Howell, February 24, 1903, in *Letters*, III, 431. For what is perhaps the fullest personal expression of Roosevelt's view of his southern appointments policy, see TR to John Graham Brooks, November 13, 1908, *ibid.*, VI, 1343–
48, in which he replies to Alfred Holt Stone's *Studies in the American Race Problem*,
an indictment of Roosevelt's attitude toward blacks.

28. See Seth M. Scheiner, "President Theodore Roosevelt and the Negro, 1901–
1908," *Journal of Negro History*, XLVII (July, 1962), 169–82; and Haney, "Theodore Roosevelt and Afro-Americans, 1901–1912."

29. TR to Henry Cabot Lodge, December 4, 1916, in *Letters*, VIII, 1132.

30. TR to Owen Wister, April 27, 1906, *ibid.*, V, 226–28.

ward" race whose close proximity to more advanced white Americans inevitably created problems. These problems would be met in the general spirit of uplift. Whites had an obligation to act as stewards or guardians for the inferior race in order to benefit both: "The only safe principle upon which Americans can act is that of 'all men up,' not that of 'some men down.'" Raising the standards of intelligence, morality, and thrift among "colored men" meant that white standards would climb "to an even higher degree." Similarly, "debasement" of blacks led to the debasement of whites.

A special problem existed, however, when society sought to "adjust the relations between two races of different ethnic type [so] that the rights of neither be abridged nor jeopardized." The backward race, Roosevelt cautioned, must be "trained so that it may enter into the possession of true freedom, while the forward race is enabled to preserve unharmed the high civilization wrought out by its forefathers." The white man must also be "trained" because he had a "well nigh unparalleled sociological responsibility." White men should remember that blacks must be trained in the long run to rely upon their own efforts for uplift and to understand that every "vicious, venal or ignorant colored man" posed a greater threat to his own race than to whites. The able black man should be included in "that share in the political work of the country which is warranted by his individual ability and integrity and the position he has won for himself." The most important need, however, was for the black race to receive "moral and industrial uplifting."[31]

Roosevelt strongly believed that education provided the key to uplift. "A perfectly stupid race can never rise to a very high plane," he declared. "The negro, for instance has been kept down by lack of intellectual development as by anything else."[32] The Lamarckian theory required him to posit the eventual susceptibility of blacks to improvement through education, but while blacks evolved and proceeded toward the social efficiency which constituted the goal of every race, whites

31. TR, "The Negro Problem," in *Works*, XVIII, 464–65.
32. TR, review of *Social Evolution* by Benjamin Kidd, in *Works*, XIV, 127.

were bound to maintain social control so as to guide the "up-lifting" of the weaker race without endangering the preservation of their own race. Education seemed to offer both a gradual approach and the best solution to the "negro problem."

Roosevelt generally subscribed to the idea that some form of industrial or technical education provided the "best type of education for the colored man, taken as a whole."[33] Still, the mechanics and home economics which would suffice for most blacks needed to be supplemented by higher education for the few. In 1911, writing to Harvey L. Simmons, a member of the board of trustees of Fisk University, Roosevelt revealed his philosophy of the educability of blacks and the need for various forms of education for both white and black.

> You do not need to be told how emphatically I favor industrial education for the colored man no less than for the white; but I cordially agree with Booker Washington in his support of Fisk, because it is eminently undesirable that the negro should have only a chance to get technical education in industry and agriculture. With the negro, as with the white, while such training is that of which there is fundamentally the greatest need for the greatest number, it is yet imperative for the sake of the race that there shall be opportunity of furnishing the different type of training for a certain proportion of the race.[34]

In preaching education to southern black people as a way to meliorate the hardships of their existence, Roosevelt made several basic assumptions. First, he assumed that technical education would well serve both whites and blacks in the "New South" and provide a source of skilled labor for white industry. Second, he concluded that in a changing and thoroughly hostile region, skilled blacks would fare better than unskilled. Third, he argued that education would decrease the extent of black lawlessness and thus of much white violence.

Roosevelt offered conventional explanations for the allegedly high crime rate among blacks. Ignoring environmental factors and the existence of a double standard for blacks, he

33. TR, *State Papers as Governor and President*, in *Works*, XVII, 416.
34. TR to Harvey L. Simmons, May 24, 1911, in *Letters*, VII, 270.

singled out laziness and shiftlessness for special condemnation and described crime and vice as "evils more potent for harm to the black race than all acts of oppression of white men put together." As incredible as this pronouncement may have seemed to blacks living in a white-dominated society, Roosevelt added insult to injury by declaring that blacks themselves had a special responsibility to police the race in order to remove these greatest threats to black progress. In Roosevelt's scheme of things, the "colored man" who failed to condemn crime in his fellows and who failed to cooperate in "bringing colored criminals to justice," was "the worst enemy of his own people as well as an enemy to all the people." [35] Yet, true to his notions of justice, Roosevelt argued that color should not be considered in punishing criminals: "The individual, not the race, must be held responsible for the crime, and this must be recognized alike by the race to which the criminal belongs and the race to which the victim belongs." [36]

If refusal to police the race dismayed Roosevelt, the mere mention of blacks acting in concert politically or otherwise aroused him even more. Although he consistently spoke out for treating blacks as individuals and condemned whites in the South who treated "each negro primarily as a negro and not individually as a man," he resolutely refused to countenance collective efforts by blacks in matters where alleged crimes were involved. In Roosevelt's mind collective action made more believable the traditional southern argument that "negroes as a race always stand by their own criminals." [37] Nothing like "race solidarity" could be allowed "in either punishing or shielding" criminals—only in catching criminals. [38]

Roosevelt feared that "race solidarity" would inevitably inflame the passion of lynch mobs at a time when lynching had increased dramatically and had become a potent national political issue. Mob action in general could not fit in Roosevelt's

---

35. TR, "The Negro," in *Works*, XVIII, 465.
36. TR to James Alexander Hemenway, June 17, 1907, in *Letters*, V, 691.
37. TR to Lyman Abbott, May 10, 1908, *ibid.*, VI, 1026.
38. TR to James Alexander Hemenway, June 17, 1907, *ibid.*, V, 691.

belief system since he so passionately proclaimed the principle of treating blacks as individuals and the affiliated idea
that whites had a special obligation to be guardians of blacks
through their period of racial development. The lynching of
blacks also offended Roosevelt's moral sensibilities because of
his tendency to view life in manichean terms and to see lynching as unmitigated "evil."

Roosevelt's attitude toward lynchings had developed as early
as his tenure as president of the New York City Police Board.
Replying in the mid-1890s to charges that he had too strenuously enforced the law, Roosevelt argued that those who made
the charges partook of the same spirit which "brings about and
is responsible for lynchings, and for all the varieties of White-
cap outrages. The men who head a lynching-party and the officials who fail to protect criminals threatened with lynching,"
he argued, "always advance as their excuse that public sentiment sanctions their action." [39] Roosevelt knew that few whites
were ever lynched and on one occasion refused to pardon a
white man charged with killing his wife, stating to Philander
Knox, "Every pardon of a murderer who should have been ex-
ecuted is to my mind just so much encouragement to lynching,
just so much putting of a premium upon lawlessness. In this
case of Hill's, if, instead of being a white man killing his wife,
he had been a negro killing a white woman with whom he had
quarreled, he would in all probability have been lynched out
of hand, and very possibly have been burnt alive." [40]

Although his denunciation of lynching may have seemed
unequivocal, Roosevelt accepted the conventional wisdom that
the cause of many lynchings was white outrage occasioned by
black assaults on white women. For example, he wrote in a
personal letter that in two recent speeches to "colored" associations he had stressed four points. First, he admonished, "At all
hazards, the brute who committed rape must be hunted down."
Second, Roosevelt declared that the black race should "take
the lead in hunting him down as practically the worst offender

39. TR, *Campaigns and Controversies*, in *Works*, XVI, 268.
40. TR to Philander Chase Knox, July 24, 1903, in *Letters*, III, 528.

against itself." Third, lynching "merely aggravated" the situation; and last, whites should "put down lynching because it was really a crime against their own race."[41] These convictions undeniably limited the effect of any purposeful action he might have taken in attempting to cope with the brutal force of Judge Lynch.

In an attempt to lead public opinion on the matter, Roosevelt wrote a long and widely publicized letter to Governor Winfield T. Durbin of Indiana. Durbin had halted a three-day race riot in Evansville in 1903 and the president wrote to congratulate him and to summarize his views on lynching. In the letter the president condemned the black man who committed the "crime horrible beyond description," arguing that the brute not only sinned against humanity, but especially against his own race as well. "Therefore," he added, "in such cases the colored people throughout the land should in every possible way show their belief that they, more than all others in the community, are horrified at the commission of such a crime and are peculiarly concerned in taking every possible measure to prevent its recurrence and to bring the criminal to immediate justice." Repeating the adjuration to "police the race," he proclaimed that "the slightest lack of vigor either in denunciation of the crime or in bringing the criminal to justice, is itself unpardonable."[42]

Thus, while he rejected lynching as a tool for social control of blacks, Roosevelt subscribed to the notion behind its justification—the idea that the rape of white women was primarily a crime perpetrated by blacks. His rejection of any concept bordering on race solidarity and his attempt to encourage blacks to inform on each other revealed his concern that blacks, as a group, posed a serious threat to white "order."

Roosevelt's understanding of the need for social control of blacks seemed perfectly logical to him and indeed was consistent with his beliefs regarding the overall "backward" status of some races. The Brownsville, Texas, incident of 1906 in which

41. TR to John William Fox, October 17, 1899, *ibid.*, II, 1085.
42. TR to Winfield Taylor Durbin, August 6, 1903, *ibid.*, III, 540.

three companies of black troops were charged with "shooting up" the Texas town illustrated how he adjusted his principles of equal treatment for individuals to the special conditions which he prescribed for black behavior.

After the midnight disturbance on August 13 and 14, 1906, local residents charged that black troops stationed at nearby Fort Brown were responsible. Antiblack feeling in the community had run high for several weeks as rumors circulated that a black soldier had "assaulted" a white woman. Although an "unofficial" group of Brownsville citizens heard testimony on the incident and affixed blame on the black soldiers, a grand jury assembled to investigate the incident could not return an indictment. Nevertheless, Roosevelt dispatched a commission of three men to investigate the matter. Their report, based almost totally upon circumstantial evidence, convinced Roosevelt that dismissal of the troops "without honor" was justified. In the ensuing protest against the summary dismissal, Roosevelt incurred the wrath of nearly all of the nation's prominent black newspapers and also took heavy criticism from many blacks who had previously supported him.[43] In addition, he began a lengthy controversy over the matter with Ohio Senator James Foraker, who thought Roosevelt's actions wholly uncalled for. The president's treatment of the black troops recalled his earlier dealings with the black soldiers with whom he had served in Cuba and suggested that he maintained his belief that black soldiers could be unpredictable and unmanageable and that groups of blacks must be "managed," even though individuals could be treated differently.

Still, President Roosevelt consistently professed to be colorblind with regard to the alleged acts of the black troops, vowing that he would have acted with precisely the same dispatch and commitment had the soldiers been white. Light is shed on Roosevelt's subsequent actions—the court martial and summary dismissal of the troops—if considered within the frame-

43. For a discussion of the events leading up to the dismissal of the troops, see Ann J. Lane, *The Brownsville Affair: National Crisis and Black Reaction* (Port Washington, New York, 1971).

work of his racial rhetoric and ideology. The president expected blacks as an immature race to behave as directed—obeying the law, helping to locate offenders within the race, and disavowing anything which even remotely resembled race solidarity—all elements of behavior which befitted a "backward race." The alleged action of the blacks had severely upset his expectations for black behavior and nearly every element of his ideological code for black behavior had been violated: blacks had broken the law as a group, had refused to identify the "guilty," and had acted in a manner which Roosevelt interpreted as race solidarity.

Later charges that Roosevelt had mistreated the blacks because of their race concerned him and he sought to dispel the notion. A year after the affair he discussed methods of convincing blacks that he had acted without special regard to color with Senator James A. Hemenway, a member of the Senate committee which investigated the incident.[44] Although Roosevelt was amenable to such an effort (Hemenway had suggested it in conversation), he remained adamant that the troops be punished and stressed that he had punished them as individuals, not as Negroes. Once more he repeated: "The individual, not the race, must be held responsible for the crime, and this must be recognized alike by the race to which the criminal belongs and the race to which the victim belongs."[45]

Although the Brownsville affair continued to disturb Roosevelt after he left the presidency, he never altered his fundamental convictions about his judgments in the matter; his personality and lifelong beliefs about the proper roles for blacks in American society militated against any acknowledgment of possible error on his part. As he vacated the White House in 1909 Roosevelt may have been glad to leave behind such nettlesome issues, but even though the presidential years had

44. Hemenway eventually believed that insufficient evidence existed to determine guilt in the matter. See Lane, *The Brownsville Affair*, 37.
45. TR to James Alexander Hemenway, June 17, 1907, in *Letters*, V, 690–91; Elliott Rudwick, *Race Riot at East St. Louis* (Carbondale, Illinois, 1964).

been full of contention and dispute his interests in blacks did not diminish. Time now allowed for a return to more theoretical speculation.

Most of Roosevelt's last years were spent in traveling and writing. Extended trips outside the United States offered opportunities for gathering more information about blacks and other nonwhites and on these jaunts the former president showed a zeal for observing and recording details and habits of blacks which matched the intensity of his childhood observation of wildlife. Roosevelt systematically observed blacks in Africa and Latin America. While he found Africans as a group backward and primitive, his curiosity and open-mindedness about unfamiliar cultures allowed him to recognize that complex social strata existed among these blacks as he noted that some, particularly Muslims "regarded themselves as of an elevated racial status, and openly looked down on the natives who were still in the kirtle-of-banana-leaves cultural stage." Among Roosevelt's attendants on his famous African safari in 1910 were "file-toothed cannibals" and other blacks who represented, in his mind, distinctly lower cultural stages. Most of his African companions were "like children, with a grasshopper inability for continuity of thought and realization of the future."

> They would often act with an inconsequence that was really puzzling. Dog-like fidelity, persevered in for months, would be ended by a fit of resentment at something unknown, or by a sheer volatility which made them abandon their jobs when it was more to their detriment than to ours. They appreciated justice, but they were neither happy nor well behaved unless they were under authority; weakness toward them was even more ruinous than harshness and over-severity.

Convinced of the need to supervise and discipline his African porters, much as he would discipline a child or any "backward race," the former president nevertheless disclosed that he, unlike his son Kermit who accompanied him on the trip, "was apt to become amused and therefore too lenient in dealing with grasshopper-like failings—which was bad for the grasshoppers themselves." [46] Traveling through Africa was like traveling through time. "I went on down the Nile through stage after stage . . . into the stage of the barbarism that was a menace to the civilization of Ptolemy and Ramses." During the trip he reflected that he had been in a "region of absolutely naked savagery among savages by no means as advanced as the early paleologic men of Europe—men living substantially the unchanged life of our infinitely remote ancestors, two hundred thousand years ago or thereabout." [47]

Similarly, in South America and the Caribbean Roosevelt found blacks in various states of cultural advancement. Although particularly intrigued by the racial hybrids he observed, he also was attracted to the physical appearance and the social customs of some Latin American blacks. In the Caribbean he admired the "powerful, finely built black woman, and little, comely brown women who strode along the paths and highroads, erect and supple, all their burdens, great or small, poised on their heads," and he explicitly noted "a tall, pretty mulatress with a little green-and-blue parrot on her shoulder." He was intrigued by the residents of Trinidad, who "like true Creoles . . . danced with ardor all night long," and he was impressed with how "very pretty some of the dark Creole girls were." He noted the varying color distinctions in Latin America and took special interest in places where sharp "social color lines are drawn not only between white and colored—as all shades of crossblood are called—but between colored and black," and places where blacks and browns held high social and political positions. Everywhere Roosevelt observed the populations "ethnically mixed" and everywhere "save in Cuba and Porto Rico" he observed that "the negroes . . . immensely outnumber the whites." [48]

Racial intermixture fascinated Roosevelt. Traveling to Brazil in 1914, he reported startling differences regarding Brazilian

46. TR, "Wild Hunting Companions," in *Works*, IV, 119–21.
47. TR, "A Zoological Trip Through Africa," lecture at Throup Polytechnic Institute, Pasadena, California, March 21, 1911, in Roosevelt Collection, Library of Congress.
48. TR, "Where the Steady Trade-Winds Blow," in *Works*, IV, 286, 308, 293.

and American views on the mixing of races to readers of the *Outlook*.[49] Aware of the controversial nature of the reportage and the American phobia about racial intermixture, the editors prefaced Roosevelt's article with a disclaimer: "It may be noted that in this article Mr. Roosevelt is not attempting either to justify or condemn the Brazilian attitude toward the Negro as contrasted with that of the United States, but simply to set forth clearly what the Brazilian attitude is in fact."

"If I were asked to name the one point in which there is complete difference between the Brazilians and ourselves," Roosevelt began, "I should say that it was in the attitude toward the black man." The principal difference which Roosevelt stressed was that blacks were "absorbed" into the population in Brazil, and that interracial sex constituted a fact of life. "My observation," he noted, "leads me to believe that in 'absorb' I have used exactly the right expression to describe this process. It is the Negro who is being absorbed and not the Negro who is absorbing the white man." Of paramount importance to Roosevelt was this latter point because he had believed since he developed the racial philosophy of history expressed in *The Winning of the West* that of necessity better types must prevail over the less desirable so that the process of progress in history could continue.

Brazil differed from America in other ways. Roosevelt related that he had met one or two "colored Deputies," a black professor and a "colored doctor," all "accepted quite simply on their worth, and apparently nobody had any idea of discriminating against them in any official or business relation because of their color." While most of the "colored people—that is, the mulattoes and quadroons"—did not rise to high social positions, he observed many "Negroes, many colored men working side by side in the same organization with whites." Even in the "higher ranks" of society no prejudice existed against marriage between whites and individuals with a "negligible" amount of black blood. Then in a remarkable observation Roosevelt de-

49. TR, "Brazil and the Negro," *Outlook*, 106 (February 21, 1914), 409–11.

scribed a painting he had viewed in Rio de Janeiro. "It portrayed a black grandfather, a mulatto son, and a white grandchild," Roosevelt observed, "the evident intention of the painter being to express both the hope and the belief that the Negro was being absorbed and transformed so that he would become a white man." Regardless of the artist's intent, Roosevelt characteristically saw the most basic principles of his own racial philosophy and beliefs in the painting.

The former president knew that his report of Brazilian racial mores could excite or provoke resentment in America, so he appended a passage to the article, which nervously reaffirmed traditional American distaste for racial intermixture. While the ideals of the two nations with regard to "treatment of the Negroes" differed greatly, in the United States the "best men," white *and* black, believed "in the complete separation of the races so far as marriage is concerned, while they also believe in treating each man of whatever color absolutely on his worth as a man, allowing him full opportunity to achieve the success warranted by his ability and integrity, and giving to him the full measure of respect to which that success entitles him." In spite of these generous sentiments, Roosevelt left no doubt that he believed Negro blood to be inferior blood, that "white" races had to guard closely against ultimate absorption by blacks. With fealty paid to the American fear of "miscegenation" he reported how Brazilians believed that blacks would not racially swamp the white race. Although some Americans thought Brazilians a "mongrel" people, the Brazilians themselves anticipated the disappearance of the Negro through "gradual absorption into the white race." Probably no "mongrelizing" would take place, he agreed, since the Brazilians, "a white people, belonging to the Mediterranean race," would continue to dominate their nation's racial character because of numbers and because of their admirable fertility rate even if more black blood were introduced. White immigration and the complete absence of black immigration also helped to account for this favorable state of affairs. "This very large European immigration of itself tends, decade by decade, to make the Negro blood a smaller element of the blood of the whole community," he concluded, a circumstance which, he observed, the "thoughtful statesmen" of Brazil applauded heartily.

The traveling former president based his conviction regarding the ability of the Brazilian to absorb the black man upon not only personal observations but also on some of the most widely held scientific theories regarding racial intermixture. In the mulatto, Roosevelt believed, neither black nor white ever persisted "in its purity." If, however, "the mulatto breeds either to the white or to the black, there will come in time a practically complete elimination of the traits of the single remote ancestor of the other blood."[50]

Roosevelt's exposure to African and Caribbean blacks came late in life after the period of his greatest political influence. To a noticeable degree, the Brazilian experiences in particular suggested to him that blacks might be physically absorbed or assimilated into the American population, like the Indian and the European immigrants whom he believed were losing or had lost their racial identities in an American melting pot. Why then, in addition to the historical American antipathy toward "miscegenation," could not Americans emulate the Brazilians and "absorb" the Negro thus eliminating the "problem"? Probably the principal answer lay in Roosevelt's belief that race suicide threatened old-stock Americans and thus their breeding powers were insufficient to absorb the black race. Nevertheless, convinced of the theoretical validity of the Brazilian experience, he may have at least toyed with the notion of racial intermixture as one way of solving American race problems, a solution which would have meshed nicely with his understanding of racial theory. Social and intellectual restraints, the apparent loss of virility among old-stock Americans, and old age inhibited him from taking these theories any further.

In spite of this brief flirtation with the idea of black/white intermixture Roosevelt, throughout his life, conceived of American blacks as belonging to an inferior race, destined to wait on

50. *Ibid.*, 409–10; TR to Henry Fairfield Osborn, December 21, 1908, in *Letters*, VI, 1436.

the process of evolution for political assimilation into American society. His standards of judgment in this category, however, were qualified by his argument that some blacks had evolved sufficiently to warrant their participation in the American polity. While these blacks had theoretically acquired characteristics which permitted them to exercise the rights of citizens, by no means could they expect to be "assimilated" racially into society, as European races and the American Indian had. In this sense, blacks always remained outcasts in the mind of Theodore Roosevelt.

CHAPTER VI

Race, Immigration, and Imperialism

During Roosevelt's lifetime Americans emerged from the security of a century's isolation to encounter a number of new "races" both at home and abroad. Whether the strangers were victims of American imperialism or whether they were part of the wave of late-nineteenth-century immigration to America, their behavior and their relation to "old-stock" Americans was often explained in terms of racial theory. In the late 1880s and 1890s the dramatic migration of millions of "new immigrants" aroused suspicion, apprehension, and a wave of antiforeign protest. Hostile sentiment ranged from that of the sophisticated Boston Brahmins with their genteel strictures about the "racial" threat, to the cacophonic prattling of the cruder and more vocal xenophobes. Out of this context of fear and misunderstanding a new nativism arose with a broad assortment of racial and religious hates which soon came to dominate the American attitude toward foreigners.

Throughout these years Theodore Roosevelt promoted the notion that immigration problems could be solved and nativism minimized if the breeding powers of the old-stock Americans remained strong enough to enable them to absorb the great masses of new people. Professing an undying belief in the "melting pot" theory and trumpeting as always the rhetoric of democracy, Roosevelt celebrated the concept of America as a repository of hope for the world's oppressed and displaced. Yet while he may have restrained from indulging in the public orgy of anti-Catholicism, anti-Semitism, and unrestrained xenophobia of the late nineteenth century, he found himself accused of nativism. Severely stung by these accusations, he told liberal reformer Carl Schurz that there was "a touch of comedy" about attacking as "'illiberal,' 'nativist,' and 'know nothing'" a man who had not "a drop of that kind of blood." Nativism was "alien to [his] whole nature."[1] He treated each man "exactly alike"; discrimination of any sort because of "creed or nativity" struck him as "infamy."[2] Still, the sharp denials cannot conceal the fact that Roosevelt, like most native-born Americans of the time, showed occasional symptoms of anti-Semitic and anti-Catholic prejudices and nativism.

Roosevelt did find militant political anti-Semitism implausible, even reprehensible, and he made many political gestures such as the appointment of Oscar Straus as secretary of commerce to highlight his belief that Jewish people should participate in national life. In addition, he took strong steps in the international arena to condemn such outrages as the massacre of large numbers of Jews at Kishinev in 1903. Yet Roosevelt made many comments which suggested that though he eschewed the more extreme representations of anti-Semitism, he had not escaped the assumptions and stereotypes of the more common variety. He remarked to a friend in 1897 on a European voyage that he had been continually annoyed by some "noisy German Jews and diseased looking South Americans" on shipboard.[3] On another occasion he spoke of finding the "right type" of Jew to fill a government post, with the querulous complaint that such "high-class Jews as Nathan Bijur, Oscar Straus and Edwin Epstein" protested another Jewish appointment to high office.[4] Roosevelt's stereotyped notion of Jews also appeared in his complaint of 1897 about the hold that "Jew money-lenders in Paris" had upon Cuban finances[5] and in his expressed hope that young Jewish men should look to individuals like Straus as a model rather than to "some crooked Jew money-maker."[6]

1. TR to Carl Schurz, July 13, 1895, in *Letters*, I, 465–66.
2. TR to Maria Longworth Storer, May 18, 1900, *ibid.*, II, 1299.
3. TR to Mrs. Helen Waldron, May 28, 1897, in Roosevelt Collection, Library of Congress.
4. TR to Frederick Norton Goddard, November 7, 1904, in *Letters*, IV, 1015.
5. TR to Ensor Chadwick, November 4, 1897, *ibid.*, I, 707.
6. TR to Lyman Abbott, May 29, 1908, *ibid.*, VI, 1042.

On the other hand, Roosevelt expressed the belief that Jewish children generally turned out to be "very much brighter" than Americans or "any other foreigner," while the Irish were "rather low down."[7] Although he had poked fun at Brooks Adams' irrational fear of Jewish bankers, noting how the younger Adams "looked forward with fiendish satisfaction to the enslavement of everybody by the Jews and other capitalists," he confided to his sister Anna that he had attended a "huge lunch [given] by the Seligmans, where at least half the guests were Jew bankers." "I felt," he reported, "as if I was personally realizing all of Brooks Adams' gloomiest anticipations of our gold-ridden, capitalist-bestridden, usurer-mastered future."[8]

Although Roosevelt repeatedly disparaged extreme anti-Semitism, he often made observations about Jewishness which suggested that he believed Jews constituted a race subject to the laws of Lamarckian evolution like any other race. He thought it would be a "particularly good thing for men of the Jewish race" to emulate "the Maccabee or fighting Jewish type."[9] "The great bulk of the Jewish population," he observed, "especially the immigrants from Russia and Poland, are of weak physique, and have not yet gotten far enough away from their centuries of oppression and degradation" to become a physically strong race. A few Jews, however, had acquired a physical prowess superior to other members of their race which made them "excellent material." Superior physical types included "the Jew who has been a gripman, or the driver of an expresswagon, or a guard on the Elevated, or the indoor Jew of fine bodily powers who has taken to boxing, wrestling, and the like."[10]

Such fine "racial" distinctions commonly occur in all of Roosevelt's racial theory. Although he did not report any observations about "indoor" Catholics, his attitudes toward anti-Catholicism and Catholics bore some similarity to his attitudes

7. TR to Robert H. Schauffler, February 2, 1912, *ibid.*, VII, 494.
8. TR to John Hay, June 17, 1899, *ibid.*, II, 1021; TR to Anna Roosevelt Cowles, November 13, 1896, *ibid.*, I, 566.
9. TR to Madison Grant, December 30, 1918, *ibid.*, VIII, 1419; TR to George Briggs Aiton, May 15, 1901, *ibid.*, III, 78.
10. TR, *Campaigns and Controversies*, in *Works*, XVI, 328–29.

toward anti-Semitism and Jews. While Roosevelt expressed strong reservations about the anti-Catholic element of American nativism and was never persuaded by the absurd notions that the Catholic Church constituted a dangerous threat to Protestant traditions and institutions, in early life he displayed an anti-Irish bias with strong overtones of anti-Catholicism. As a young representative in the New York legislature during the 1880s, Roosevelt savagely satirized the Irish representatives and especially condemned the Catholic Irish. Most were "vicious, stupid looking scoundrels with apparently not a redeeming trait, beyond the capacity for making exceeding ludicrous bulls," Roosevelt wrote in January, 1882. One Tammany representative—"a little celtic liquor seller, about five feet high, with an enormous stomach, and a face like a bull frog"—especially offended the youthful Roosevelt's patrician sense of decorum, and he took care to record an exchange between this Irishman and the clerk of the house.

Bogan.   "Mr. Clur-rk!"
Clerk.   "The gentleman from New York, Mr. Bogan."
Bogan.   "I rise to a pint of ardther (order) under the rules."
Clerk.   "There are no rules."
Bogan.   "Thin I object to thim!"
Clerk.   "There are no rules to object to."
Bogan.   (meditatively) "Indade! That's quare, now; (brightening up as he sees a way out of the difficulty) Viry will! Thin I move that they be amended till there ar-r-r!" (smiles complacently on the applauding audience, proudly conscious that he has at last solved an abstruse point of parliamentary practice.)

Although he esteemed a few of the second-generation Irish, Roosevelt found most of the House's twenty-five Irish Democrats a "stupid, sodden vicious lot . . . equally deficient in brains and virtue." Among these he found the "average catholic [sic] Irishman of the first generation as represented in this Assembly" to be "a low, venal, corrupt and unintelligent brute." One member of the House he assayed with the following description:

The Chairman is an Irishman named Murphy, Colonel in the Civil War, a Fenian; he is a tall stout man, with a swollen red face, a black moustache, and a ludicrously dignified manner; always wears a frock coat (very shiney) and has had a long experience in politics—so that to undoubted pluck and a certain knowledge of parliamentary forms, he adds a great deal of stupidity and a decided looseness of ideas as regards the 8th commandment.

A Brooklyn representative more favorably impressed the young legislator since he was "Americanized more fully." Roosevelt characterized another Irishman as a "vicious little, Celtic nonentity from Buffaloe [*sic*]," and still another as, "either dumb or an idiot." One "Tammany Hall gentleman named MacManus," Roosevelt sniffed, was "a huge, fleshy, unutterably coarse and low brute . . . formerly a prize fighter, [who] at present keeps a low drinking and dancing saloon, and is more than suspected of having begun his life as a pick pocket."[11]

Roosevelt regarded the "Presbyterian Irish" (the Scotch-Irish) with a great deal more approval,[12] because of his Scotch-Irish ancestry and of his admiration for the Scotch-Irish frontiersmen. Generally, however, he softened even his private anti-Irish sentiments soon after his tenure in the New York Legislature, probably because of his growing awareness of the political power of New York's Irishmen.

In fact, Roosevelt carried on occasional campaigns against anti-Catholicism which suggested he had a clear awareness of the political dividends which could be earned. His campaigns against anti-Catholicism earned him much support from Catholic immigrants, just as his public attitudes toward blacks were often well received among Afro-Americans. Virtue and self-interest met in each instance to win him favor among both groups. Writing his sister Anna in the fall of 1882, he chided a friend who "shows a strong tendency to trace all evils from the absence of rain to the fight with the Arabi Pascha, to the presence of Roman Catholics in America."[13]

11. TR, "Diary of Five Months in the New York Legislature," in *Letters*, II, 1469–71.
12. See Chapter III herein and *The Winning of the West, passim*.
13. TR to Anna Roosevelt, September 15, 1882, in *Letters*, I, 56–57.

As early as his Civil Service Commission years Roosevelt frequently stressed his resolve to appoint men to office without regard for their religious beliefs. The enthusiasm with which he proclaimed his opposition to intolerance suggests that he was aware of the political dividends which this posture paid. "The Know-Nothing Movement," Roosevelt declared in the 1890s, "in every form is entirely repugnant to true Americanism and this is, perhaps, especially the case when it is directed not merely against American citizens of foreign origin, but also against even native-born Americans of a different creed." No distinction with respect to "creed" or "race origin" had been made "on the roll of honor where we have engraved the names of the nation's statesmen and soldiers, patriots and commonwealth-builders," young Roosevelt declared. What man, he asked, "with a particle of patriotic spirit" would care whether General Sherman had been a Protestant or Sheridan a Catholic? Thus his denunciation of anti-Catholicism often appeared in fervent, nationalist garb and tended to serve patriotism a little more than religious toleration.[14]

Nevertheless, TR did not always make toleration serve other purposes. Late in his life in private correspondence as well as public assertion he opposed virulent anti-Catholics, as in the case of his exchange of letters with the Catholic-hating Georgia politician Tom Watson (who thought of the Pope as a "fat old Dago").[15] He passionately declaimed against Watson's diatribes and sought to dissuade the Georgia politician from his radical anti-Catholic views. "I am deeply disappointed at the violent feeling you seem to have against your Catholic fellow-citizens," Roosevelt informed Watson in 1915 and added "I do not regard such a feeling as compatible with a real and full belief in our American institutions."[16] A few months later he also

14. TR, *American Ideals*, in *Works*, XV, 34–35.
15. Quoted in Charles Crowe, "Tom Watson, Populists, and Blacks Reconsidered," *Journal of Negro History*, LV (1970), 99.
16. TR to Thomas E. Watson, January 19, 1915, in Roosevelt Collection, Library of Congress. Also see Thomas G. Dyer, "Aaron's Rod: Theodore Roosevelt, Tom Watson and Anti-Catholicism," Washington State University *Research Studies* (March, 1976), 60–68.

condemned Watson's suggestion that public schools should exclude Catholics and stressed that schools should be open to all "creeds."[17]

Just as Roosevelt managed to hold in check most of his anti-Semitic and anti-Catholic inclinations, so too he sought to temper antiforeign urges which arose from concern about the "new" immigration. His interest in the social dynamics of immigration was broad and wide-ranging and he regularly examined the United States census in attempts to understand more about the movement of immigrants into the country and what happened to them after they arrived. For a while in 1893 Roosevelt considered joining Henry Cabot Lodge in a study which would focus on "the distribution of immigrants throughout the country, with the curious differences shown in the different localities to which the different races go, the number of paupers and criminals they furnish, and the general bearing of the statistics upon the problem of controlling immigration."[18] Although he did not pursue the matter, the inquiry stimulated his tendency to judge the worth of various immigrant groups. While the Irish to him represented some of the more undesirable immigrants who had come to America, Roosevelt had only praise for other groups. He found, for example, that the "Huguenots and Puritans and the German 'Forty-eighters' were on the whole the three best stocks that came here." Of the three, he inclined toward the belief that "German immigration is a little better than any other."[19]

During the great immigration surge of the 1890s, Roosevelt accepted the idea that it would be necessary to curtail American immigration by passing "more drastic laws than now exist." Although he felt that restriction should be accomplished with the objective of protecting the American labor market, Roosevelt also observed that Americans should "keep out races which do not rapidly assimilate with our own," as well as "unworthy

17. TR to Thomas E. Watson, March 16, 1915, in Roosevelt Collection, Library of Congress.
18. TR to Richard Watson Gilder, April 1, 1893, in *Letters*, I, 311.
19. TR to Fraser Metzger, January 1, 1915, in Roosevelt Collection, Library of Congress.

individuals of all races—not only criminals, idiots, and paupers, but anarchists." [20] During his presidency Roosevelt sought
to convey these racial abstractions into law by calling repeatedly for restrictions on immigration and by urging that only the
"right type" of immigrants be admitted. [21] Generally he wished
to ban East European immigrants who were "anarchists" and
those who could not demonstrate through "a careful and not
merely perfunctory educational test some intelligent capacity
to appreciate American institutions and act sanely as American
citizens." [22] Unspoken at this time was the general notion that
Orientals should be excluded altogether.

The reasons for his support of restriction relate to apprehen-
sions about the social and political problems that seemed to
flow from the presence of large numbers of fresh immigrants.
A developing fear of race suicide, a concomitant reverence for
the old stock, a belief that many of the "new immigrants" possessed alien habits which were not rapidly changed, and a sensitivity to the popularity of immigration restriction as a political issue pushed him toward the idea of exclusion. Political
implications particularly concerned the ambitious Roosevelt
in 1897, when he querulously complained to Lodge that to his
"horror" the New York *Sun* "yesterday put me down as opposed to the restriction of immigration; this being the way they
had construed an ardent appeal of mine to the labor union men
to restrict it." He quickly added: "I corrected it in the *Sun* of
this morning." [23]

While Roosevelt sought to exploit politically the immigration restriction issue he avoided extreme expressions of antiforeign sentiments. To surrender to the more blatant forms of
nativism would have constituted an admission that the great
principle of assimilation which stood at the heart of his racial
theory was no longer operative and that the melting-pot notion, the key element in his assimilationist rhetoric, had lost

20. TR, "True Americanism," in *Works*, XV, 27, 15–31.
21. TR, *State Papers as Governor and President*, in *Works*, XVII, 204.
22. *Ibid.*, 111.
23. TR to Henry Cabot Lodge, January 30, 1897, in *Letters*, I, 576.

validity. Roosevelt's tenacious and well-known support of the assimilation idea led Israel Zangwill to dedicate his famous play, "The Melting Pot" to TR. Some years after the production of the play Zangwill wrote the former president to inquire if he still believed in the concept. A strong reaffirmation of the notion soon followed.

> But, my dear Sir, the idea that I have forgotten the "Melting Pot," and its dedication to me! Now as a matter of fact that particular play I shall always count among the very strong and real influences upon my thought and my life. It has been in my mind continually, and on my lips often during the last three years. It not merely dealt with the "melting pot," with the fusing of all foreign nationalities into an American nationality, but it also dealt with the great ideals which it is just as essential for the native born as for the foreign to realize and uphold if the new nationality is to represent a real addition to the sum total of human achievement.[24]

Roosevelt's melting pot rhetoric had always been closely tied to the notion of the fusing of Americans into one race, and he always argued that the American represented an entirely new ethnic type. The new American race was for Roosevelt an old theme which had appeared as early as 1887 in his biography of Thomas Hart Benton, which emphasized the power of the "stern and hard surroundings" of the environment in "hammer[ing] this people into a peculiar and characteristically American type." It had become apparent "before the outbreak of the Revolution," that the American people, "not only because of their surroundings, physical and spiritual, but because of the mixture of blood that had already begun to take place, represented a new and distinct ethnic type."[25] Roosevelt frequently informed his correspondents, "We are making a new race, a new type, in this country,"[26] and in his presidential address to the American Historical Association in December, 1912, he

---

24. TR to Israel Zangwill, November 27, 1912, in Roosevelt Collection, Library of Congress.
25. TR, *Thomas Hart Benton*, in *Works*, VIII, 4–5.
26. TR to Edward Grey, December 18, 1906, in *Letters*, V, 529.

forecast that future historians would tell of the "formation of a new ethnic type in this melting-pot of the nations."[27] The type, Roosevelt observed, "has never been fixed in blood," and indeed continued to change. He argued unconvincingly that for the past sixty years while "the tide of immigration had been at full," even the new immigrants had soon become "absorbed" into American life, "radically and profoundly changed thereby, the rapidity of their assimilation being marvelous." Each group of new immigrants, he observed, "adds its blood to the life" of the nation and "changes it somewhat," a process which had been going on for three centuries.[28]

Roosevelt called the assimilation process Americanization and in his thought it served as both a racial and a nationalistic concept. This "most interesting of all problems" involved the "amalgamation and assimilation of the different race strains in this country." TR himself stood as a living example of the wondrous Americanizing alchemy, the Dutch, Scotch, Irish, and other "race stocks" in his blood being "absolutely merged in an American whole." However, "curious differences" existed "between the different races" with respect to the speed with which they were assimilated. German and Scandinavian Protestants merged rather quickly with the old stock, while Catholics took longer. In fact, it appeared that Roosevelt predicted separate melting pots for Protestants and Catholics.

> When the Catholic Germans learn to speak English as their home tongue, they intermarry more or less with the Irish; and they will doubtless intermarry with the Slavonians and Italians under like conditions, when the latter begin to move upward in the social scale.

The optimistic Roosevelt departed from his more pessimistic acquaintances by forecasting that eventually *all* white immigrants would blend in the giant process of Americanization. "Complete intermixture," however, would usually take place only after the second generation had been born in America.[29]

27. TR, "History as Literature," in *Works*, XIV, 27–28.
28. TR, "The Settlement of Jamestown," in *Works*, XII, 587–88.
29. TR to Ernest Bruncken, March 1, 1898, in *Letters*, I, 786–87; TR to Thomas P. Gill, January 17, 1911, *ibid.*, VII, 209. For the Americanization process on the frontier, see *The Winning of the West*, in *Works*, X, 101.

Whereas Roosevelt argued that Americanization primarily denoted the process of absorbing immigrants into the national bloodstream, the doctrine also referred to cultural assimilation and to Anglo-conformity. Americanization became a process for homogenizing the foreign-born, for encouraging uniformity, and for discouraging behavior which did not comport with "the American way." In an article published by the *Forum* in April, 1894, on "True Americanism," he stressed that immigrants should become Americanized in politics, principles, in their "way of looking at the relations between Church and State," as well as in race. Moreover, immigrants should change their names and their customs, for to bear an American name was "to bear the most honorable of titles." Without the name change and without passing through the crucible of Americanization the immigrant in a "few generations" would become an "uncouth boor," and a "mere obstruction to national life." Immigrants should understand, Roosevelt warned, that "it is beyond all question the wise thing . . . to become thoroughly Americanized," and old-stock Americans had a right to demand it. Roosevelt concluded that "though we ourselves suffer from their perversity, it is they who really suffer most."

In the quest for conformity and a uniform culture Roosevelt had always deplored "hyphenation." While president of the police board in New York City, he displayed a powerful aversion for the retention of European cultural traits by the city's immigrants. His yearning for uniformity combined with a belief that hyphenation perpetuated diversity and obstructed assimilation and the fostering of national loyalties: "Remember, that the one being abhorrent to the powers above the earth and under them is the hyphenated American—the 'German-American,' the 'Irish-American,' or the 'native-American.' Be Americans, pure and simple." [30]

This distaste for hyphenation erupted again in the era of World War I. As a national campaign for Americanization commenced, Roosevelt led the chorus demanding that ethnics shed old ways. By that time, however, the idea had lost much of its

---

30. TR, "True Americanism," in *Works*, XV, 24–28; TR, *Campaigns and Controversies, ibid.*, XVI, 276.

earlier racial character and had acquired stronger nationalistic connotations. Just before American entry into the conflict, Roosevelt linked Americanization to the notion of preparedness, labeling the ideas as "the two paramount phases or elements of the work of constructive patriotism,"[31] and in the last letter he wrote before his death in January, 1919, he stressed again the significance of the process in both nationalistic and assimilative aspects. Because the war had ended, he wrote, there was no reason for "sagging back in the fight for Americanism." He feared that some people had already begun to plan the revival of "all the foreign associations which most directly interfere with the complete Americanization of our people." He argued that American principles in this matter "should be absolutely simple." An immigrant who came to America and "assimilates himself to us" would be treated as an equal. Assimilation only required that the immigrant become an American "and nothing but an American," forswearing all ethnic identity. To do otherwise was to fail in one's duty.

> There can be no divided allegiance here. Any man who says he is an American but something else also, isn't an American at all. We have room but for one flag, the American flag, and this excludes the red flag which symbolizes all wars against liberty and civilization just as much as it excludes any foreign flag of a nation to which we are hostile. We have room for but one language here and that is the English language, for we intend to see that the crucible turns our people out as Americans, of American nationality, and not as dwellers in a polyglot boardinghouse; and we have room for but one soul loyalty, and that loyalty is to the American people.[32]

Some non-European, nonwhite groups, however, could not pass through the crucible. Blacks, of course, did not qualify for assimilation and neither did Orientals or Latin Americans. That these groups alone differed enough racially to be excluded,

31. TR to Stanwood Menken, January 10, 1917, in *Letters*, VIII, 1143.
32. TR to Richard Melancthon Hurd, January 3, 1919, *ibid.*, VIII, 1422. For a full expression of Roosevelt's World War I beliefs about assimilation see "The Children of the Crucible," in *Works*, XXI, 35–53.

Roosevelt made clear in his stress on the ultimate eligibility of southern and eastern Europeans for membership in the select racial group. In America, he noted in 1914, "the descendants of the Slavonic immigrants become men precisely like ourselves."[33] These white immigrants, Roosevelt believed, should be imported in large numbers into Hawaii to serve as laborers so that the "coolie" element of Japanese and Chinese did not become numerically superior. Planters who ignored this race threat and imported Oriental workers were "incapable of thinking of the future of their children," Roosevelt complained, and he declared that he would do "everything [he] could to encourage the immigration of Southern Europeans to the island." So important was the problem that Europeans, "no matter of what ancestry," should be imported "in order that the islands may be filled with a white population of our general civilization and culture."[34] The immigration laws should be amended so that "tens of thousands of Spaniards, Portuguese, or Italians, or of any of the other European races" could be brought in to serve as the prime labor source.[35]

Roosevelt's objection to Japanese immigration stemmed from the belief that the predominantly white population of the United States would be unable to absorb or assimilate Orientals, and that racial differences between Orientals and whites loomed so high as to preclude even basic understanding between the two groups. "This whole Japanese business [the immigration controversy] is very puzzling," he wrote his friend Speck Von Sternberg in 1907. "I suppose because there are such deep racial differences that it is very hard for any of us of European descent to understand them or be understood by them."[36] The perplexed Roosevelt wrote his friend and confidant Cecil Spring-Rice in 1904 that "their thoughts are not our thoughts," although he admitted that he could not explain why. The explanation did not seem to lie in the "fact" that the

---

33. TR to Hugo Münsterberg, October 6, 1914, in *Letters*, VIII, 824.
34. TR to Philander Knox, February 8, 1909, *ibid.*, VI, 1512–13.
35. TR to William Kent, February 4, 1909, *ibid.*, VI, 1504.
36. TR to Hermann Speck Von Sternberg, July 16, 1907, *ibid.*, V, 720.

Japanese were a "non-Aryan race," for in recent years, he told Spring-Rice, he had come to suspect that the "non-Aryan, far-eastern Japanese were in some essentials closer to us than their chief opponents [the Russians]." The American racial relationship with the Japanese seemed to be like that with the Finns and Hungarians, who were "perhaps less akin to us by race" than the Persians yet differed no less from Americans than the "Slavonians and Croats." The Japanese were "less alien" to Americans than the "Balkan Slavs who have become Mohammedans." [37]

Despite Roosevelt's objections to Japanese immigration he professed admiration for certain of their racial qualities. In fact, he had developed a substantial regard for many aspects of Japanese character. In his opinion they seemed to have reached a reasonably high state of civilization and were in their racial prime with much confidence in their prowess and strength as a people. This judgment had rooted itself in Roosevelt's consciousness as early as 1900 when American troops joined with Japanese and European soldiers to suppress the Boxer Rebellion. The recently elected vice-president informed Von Sternberg of his respect for the fighting ability of the Japanese: "It looks to me from all I can gather as if the Japanese had done best" in the campaign. "What natural fighters they are! I am told that the Russians were the worst for plundering and murdering and that the Americans had a tendency to get drunk and to plunder but never killed women and children." [38] Later on the same day he commented enthusiastically to Spring-Rice "what extraordinary soldiers those little Japs are." [39]

In the next five years the president's admiration for the Japanese grew. For a long period he wrestled three times a week with two Japanese wrestlers, and soon he began to sing the praises not just of Japanese fighting abilities but also of their generally fine character. In 1905 he expressed the thought that "most certainly the Japs are a wonderful people . . . quite as

37. TR to Cecil Arthur Spring-Rice, January 18, 1904, *ibid.*, III, 698.
38. TR to Hermann Speck Von Sternberg, November 19, 1900, *ibid.*, II, 1428.
39. TR to Cecil Arthur Spring-Rice, November 19, 1900, *ibid.*, II, 1423.

remarkable industrially as in warfare," and likely in time to take
their place "as a great civilized power of a formidable type."
He was quick to add, however, that they would develop "with
motives and ways of thought which are not quite those of the
powers of our race."[40]

President Roosevelt's high regard for aspects of the Japanese character created substantial intellectual problems for
him when he confronted the issue of Japanese immigration. It
became necessary, for example, to justify exclusion while continuing to profess admiration for the Japanese "race." He attempted to deal with the problem by emphasizing the racial
distance between white Americans and the Orientals. While
granting that Japan's civilization stood "higher than our own"
in some respects, Roosevelt still insisted that it was "eminently
undesirable that Japanese and Americans should attempt to
live together in masses." Since mixing the "races" would inevitably end "disastrously," he advised statesmen of both countries to work for the prevention of such undesirable results.
One could not expect in only a generation or two to overcome
great racial differences, particularly differences which reached
far into the past. The historically obsessed Roosevelt wrote:

> But the lines of development . . . of the Orient and the Occident,
> have been separate and divergent since thousands of years be-
> fore the Christian era; certainly since the hoary eld in which the
> Akkadian predecessors of the Chaldean Semites held sway in
> Mesopotamia. An effort to mix together, out of hand, the peoples
> representing the culminating points of two such lines of diver-
> gent cultural development would be fraught with peril; and this,
> I repeat, because the two are different, not because either is in-
> ferior to the other.[41]

Sometimes Roosevelt took pains to emphasize the cultural
differences between Japanese and Americans, but as always
he blurred the theoretical lines between culture and race. At

40. TR to Kermit Roosevelt, March 5, 1904, *ibid.*, IV, 744; TR to Robert Grant,
March 14, 1905, *ibid.*, IV, 1140; TR to Cecil Arthur Spring-Rice, June 16, 1905, *ibid.*,
IV, 1233.
41. TR, *Autobiography*, in *Works*, XXII, 433.

other times, however, he stressed the great racial differences between the two peoples and pointed to the overwhelming importance of such differences to the development of his thought with respect to the Japanese. He informed a friend one month before leaving the White House, "Our line of policy must be adopted holding ever in view the fact that this is a race question, and that race questions stand by themselves. I did not clearly see this at the outset, but for nearly three years I have seen it, and thruout [*sic*] my treatment of the question have shaped my course accordingly." He concluded his remarks with the firmest possible statement of his belief that Japanese and Americans must not mix racially. "The one important point," Roosevelt emphasized, "is that the Japanese should, as a race, be excluded from becoming permanent inhabitants of our territory, they in return excluding us from becoming permanent inhabitants of their territory."[42] Four days later, with the subject still preying on his mind, he wrote William Howard Taft's secretary of state-designate urging him to consider the racial implications of Japanese immigration. Roosevelt warned in apocalyptic tones that "to permit the Japanese to come in large numbers into this country would be to cause a race problem and invite and insure a race contest." He concluded with the simple and blunt assertion that "it is necessary to keep them out."[43]

Roosevelt as president had indeed sought to exclude the Japanese. His primary expressed aim had been to prevent the admission of large numbers of Japanese laborers because their "very frugality, abstemiousness and clannishness make them formidable to our laboring class," a situation made even more serious "because they keep an entirely distinct and alien mass."[44] Exclusion had been accomplished by the "Gentlemen's Agreement" of 1907 but in the course of the dispute Roosevelt had seriously wounded Japanese pride despite attempts to soften the harshness of his policy by stressing that Japanese "gentlemen" and students were welcome in the United

42. TR to William Kent, February 4, 1909, in *Letters*, VI, 1503.
43. TR to Philander Chase Knox, February 8, 1909, *ibid.*, VI, 1511.
44. TR to George Kennan, May 6, 1905, *ibid.*, IV, 1168–69.

States.[45] Still, the notion remained uppermost in Roosevelt's mind that such great racial differences existed between the two peoples that any other policy would be unworkable in spite of the fact that "so many sentimentalists" could not perceive the importance of race in the affair.

While stressing the necessity for exclusion, Roosevelt condemned efforts to sequester Japanese already in the United States and regarded attempts to establish "Jim Crow" railroad cars for Japanese as "silly" and "indefensible." In addition he scolded Californians and Nevadans who sought to enact laws preventing Japanese children from attending public schools.[46] Yet he accepted the idea that Japanese men resembled blacks in a tendency to commit sexual crimes against white women and also embraced the corollary notion that these crimes were inducements to white violence against the Japanese as well as against the blacks. Thus, he wrote in April, 1908, "I can never tell when race animosity will be called into exercise by some sexual misconduct on the part of a Japanese."[47]

The Japanese "question" had presented Roosevelt with a variety of social, political, and ideological problems. He had sought to solve these by developing rationales for discrimination against the Japanese based on his understanding of racial differences between them and Americans. His concern for the racial differences he perceived, however, did not translate into a full-blown hysteria about a "yellow peril." In fact, Roosevelt was fond of pointing out that he had "never been able to make himself afraid of the 'yellow peril,'" and that the association of barbarism with yellow skin made little sense.[48] Although he sought a middle ground here as he had with respect to extreme nativism, in the final analysis his fear of the effects of widespread racial intermixture between Japanese and whites triumphed over his respect for Japanese culture.

Roosevelt did not respect the Chinese as he did the Japa-

45. See, for example, TR to John St. Loe Strachey, December 21, 1906, *ibid.*, V, 532.
46. TR to James Norris Gillett, February 4, 1909, *ibid.*, VI, 1504.
47. TR to Arthur H. Lee, April 8, 1908, *ibid.*, VI, 995.
48. TR to John C. O'Laughlin, August 31, 1905, *ibid.*, IV, 1328; TR to David B. Schneder, June 19, 1905, *ibid.*, IV, 1240.

nese and placed them in a far lower position in the stages of civilization scheme. The Chinese had fallen into racial decadence, had lost the martial virtues, and were unable to assert themselves as a people. In fact he so thoroughly deplored their racial character that he used the term "Chinese" as an epithet of opprobrium. As early as 1882 Roosevelt agreed that Chinese immigration should be curtailed. It seemed "incredible" to him that anyone of "even moderate intelligence" could fail to see that "no greater calamity could now befall the United States than to have the Pacific slope fill up with a Mongolian population." Twenty years later as president he maintained the same position except for the nominal concession of expressing willingness to admit members of Chinese middle and upper classes.[49]

Roosevelt held similarly negative opinions about the principal victims of American imperialism, Filipinos and Latin Americans. He informed Rudyard Kipling that "in dealing with the Philippines I have first [to deal with] the jack-fools who seriously think that any group of pirates and head-hunters needs nothing but independence in order that it may be turned forthwith into a dark-hued New England town meeting." With respect to the Colombians, he argued that he was dealing with a "corrupt pithecoid community" hardly entitled to the same treatment that European nations merited.[50] Roosevelt regarded both Filipinos and Latin Americans as occupants of low rungs on the civilization ladder. The Filipinos, in his view, were savages; and the leader of the Filipino independence movement, Emilio Aguinaldo, was "the typical representative of savagery, the typical foe of civilization and the American people."[51] As "backward peoples" these individuals occupied positions of inferiority in Roosevelt's scheme of things and thus were fair

---

49. TR, *Thomas Hart Benton*, in *Works*, VIII, 118; TR to Leslie M. Shaw, March 27, 1902, in *Letters*, III, 249; TR to T. C. Friedlander, November 23, 1905, *ibid.*, V, 90; TR to Henry H. D. Pierce, June 24, 1905, *ibid.*, IV, 1251; TR to Victor H. Metcalf, June 16, 1905, *ibid.*, IV, 1235.
50. TR to Rudyard Kipling, November 1, 1904, *ibid.*, IV, 1007–1008.
51. Speech of Governor Theodore Roosevelt, Cincinnati, Ohio, October 21, 1899, in Roosevelt Collection, Library of Congress.

game for American imperialistic desires. His Lamarckianism, however, required him to posit the eventual adaptability of such "races," and their ultimate ascension up the ladder of evolutionary development toward the state of "social efficiency" which characterized the higher races. Like the American black, Filipinos and Latin Americans would have to proceed through the slow process of racial evolution before acquiring the skills necessary to manage their own affairs. And like the blacks, Latin Americans and Filipinos could count upon the supervision of white "stewards" as guardians of civilization. Had America failed to "protect" the Cubans, for example, the island would have sunk "into chaos and savagery."[52] Roosevelt argued that as a general rule "no civilized power is or ever has been able permanently to keep peace" among "savage, barbarous, or semi-barbarous peoples, because these latter are not able to so conduct themselves as to render peace possible."[53] A general concomitant to this attitude which posited the victims of American imperialism as inferior races was the Rooseveltian notion that one of the primary traits of the superior races was the inclination to exercise control over "backward peoples." In 1897, just before American imperialistic desires burst upon the world, Roosevelt cast the proposed annexation of Hawaii in a sharply racial light. If Hawaii were not taken, he told Alfred T. Mahan, "it will show that we either have lost, or else wholly lack, the masterful instinct which alone can make a race great," an unthinkable circumstance for an individual who thought of the great races as possessing vigorous expansionist tendencies. "I feel so deeply about it," he told Mahan, "that I hardly dare express myself in full." Roosevelt concluded that "the terrible part is to see that it is the men of education who take the lead in trying to make us prove traitors to our race."[54]

This combination of jingoism and race thinking provided the context for Roosevelt's thoughts about imperialism. Taken

52. Speech at Hartford, Connecticut, August 22, 1902, *ibid.*
53. Speech of Governor Theodore Roosevelt, Cincinnati, Ohio, October 21, 1899, *ibid.*
54. TR to Alfred Thayer Mahan, December 11, 1897, in *Letters*, I, 741.

together with his powerful reverence for the special racial qualifications of the English-speaking race and more particularly the American "race," it becomes clear that his approach to imperialism was as racially oriented as it was nationalistically inspired. If the high tide of his imperialistic activity began to ebb during his presidency, his racial concerns continued to find expression in his attitudes toward Orientals and immigrants in general.

Thus the encounter with a wide assortment of new "races" at home and abroad ended for Roosevelt in the belief that in both instances the white American "race" should expect conformity to its culture. In the case of the immigrants conformity meant that old ways would not be tolerated and that assimilation would be the guiding principle of their existence. For Orientals and Latin Americans who found themselves victims of American imperialism the message was largely the same: Conform to American culture and political forms or expect "displacement" by the English-speaking peoples. Immigration and imperialism were thus intimately tied in Roosevelt's mind by the nexus of race; and race questions, as TR noted, "stand by themselves."

CHAPTER VII

Race Suicide

Few social science theories gripped the Western imagination more completely at the turn of the century than the idea of race suicide. In enthusiastic discussions on both sides of the Atlantic among laymen as well as scholars the concept combined much viable contemporary thought from anthropology, sociology, history, and other disciplines and stressed the notion that entire "races" of men faced extinction through failure to fulfill the reproductive function. Foremost among the true believers in this doctrine stood the American race theorist, amateur sociologist, and politician Theodore Roosevelt, who for the last thirty years of his life promoted the idea that racial extinction faced the "higher races" if they did not increase their procreative activities. Throughout these three decades, Roosevelt developed a personal theory of race suicide and sought to apply the principles of this thought in the social realm. For the scholar-politician, remedying the debility which he believed resulted from the tendency toward race suicide became an obsession.

Roosevelt's concern for the perpetuation of the qualities he so admired in the white American "race" received an initial jolt in 1892 when he closely examined the newly released census of 1890. The population count revealed to him, as it did to others with similar attitudes on race, an apparent decline in the fertility of old-stock Americans in comparison to immigrants. For some individuals like the Boston patricians described by Barbara Solomon in *Ancestors and Immigrants*, the census indicated a swamping of the old stock by the racially inferior immigrants.[1] For Roosevelt the census marked the beginning of a twenty-eight-year obsession with the maintenance and preservation of the racial integrity of old-stock Americans and indeed of all members of the "English-speaking race." Ultimately, a concern heavy with Rooseveltian morality would overflow into a number of "race suicide" issues, such as marriage, divorce, the integrity of the home, eugenics, feminism, sexual relations, and even the political issues of good citizenship, the destiny of the nation, and the future of the entire white race.

In 1892, however, Roosevelt interpreted the declining birthrate among old-stock New Englanders only in relation to the substantial numbers of French Canadians who were then settling in Massachusetts and surrounding states. "Looking over the recent census figures for New England," he wrote Francis Parkman, "It is curious, and rather melancholy to see the strange revenge which time is bringing to the French of Canada." At this point, Roosevelt regarded the French-Canadian incursion as merely "curious" because he had not developed a systematic theory of race suicide. Yet many elements of that theory were present in the letter to Parkman: the belief that the French Canadians were "swarming into New England with ominous rapidity," the concern that the French language might replace English here and there, and the gnawing premonition that "their race will in many places supplant the real American stock." Despite these fears the still sanguine assimilationist believed that the future would "somehow bring things right in the end for our land."[2]

If Roosevelt did not immediately sense all the implications of race suicide, scarcely two years later he had accepted other concepts which pushed him toward a fuller appreciation of the idea. These thoughts, which also provided the basis for some of his general racial theories, came at least in part from his reading of Charles Pearson's *National Life and Character* (1894), one of the many tomes of the era which sought to explain all of

---

1. Barbara Solomon, *Ancestors and Immigrants: A Changing New England Tradition* (Cambridge, Massachusetts, 1956).
2. Theodore Roosevelt to Francis Parkman, May 22, 1892, in *Letters*, I, 282–83.

human history and behavior in racial terms.[3] Pearson argued
that races and nations, like individuals, pass through various
stages of life from birth to death. In particular he stressed that
races eventually reach a "stationary state," a point where development ceased and stagnation ensued. Roosevelt accepted
this general maxim and incorporated it in his thought about the
American "race-future."

Roosevelt agreed with Pearson that the "higher orders of
every society tend to die out; that there is a tendency on the
whole, for both lower classes and lower civilizations to increase
faster than the higher." The cream of society—military com-
manders, statesmen, poets, scientists, and other great men—
simply did not sire as many children as members of the lower
classes. Thus it appeared that the upper "castes" of society and
of the race had reached the "stationary-state." Although he argued that "no community . . . actually diminishing in numbers
is in a healthy condition," the imperialistic TR felt that the need
for a fecund population was especially acute at a time when
the world's "huge waste places" needed to be filled. If Americans were to participate in world politics, they must realize
that the "competition between the races" had been reduced to
the "warfare of the cradle" and that no race had a chance "to
win a great place" unless it consisted of "good breeders as well
as good fighters." Despite a clear concern for the failure of the
upper strata of society to reproduce with the fervor of the lower
orders, Roosevelt did not yet despair for the overall condition
of the race. While he believed that it might prove very difficult
to "prevent the higher races from losing their nobler traits and
from being overwhelmed by the lower races," things did change
and a nation might still "play a great part in the world," despite
the diminished reproductive activities of its better classes.[4]

After 1894 Roosevelt became increasingly convinced that
declining birthrates spelled serious difficulties for the maintenance of the tried and tested old-stock Americans. And, as
his convictions about race suicide intensified so did his efforts

3. TR to Charles Henry Pearson, May 11, 1894, *ibid.*, I, 376–77.
4. TR, "National Life and Character," in *Works*, XIV, 248–50, 257.

to convince others of the necessity for recognizing the problem and dealing decisively with it. Already fortified with the statistics on the New England birthrate, he soon discovered to his own satisfaction that barrenness cursed France with a death rate which already exceeded the birthrate! When a race reached this position, Roosevelt thundered, "then that race is not only fated to extinction but it deserves extinction. When the capacity and desire for fatherhood and motherhood is lost the race goes down, and should go down; and we need to have the plainest kind of plain speaking addressed to those individuals who fear to bring children into the world." A race could not survive if it did not "breed well."[5]

Although the future president now accepted the theoretical possibility of race suicide and its corollaries, he only slowly became convinced that racial extinction was imminent for Americans and the "higher races" in general. Seeking answers from history, Roosevelt speculated about possible connections between the fall in birthrates and the collapse of Rome and concluded that Rome's difficulties had indeed been due to declining fertility. The empire, it seemed, fell "because there sprang from its loins no children to defend it against the barbarians."[6] Cecil Spring-Rice suggested that other causes also must be considered, including the indiscriminate introduction into Rome of lower races. Roosevelt agreed that "a change in the population itself caused by the immense importation of slaves, usually of inferior races," had helped to doom the empire but he insisted that failure of the best stock to reproduce had sealed its fate. Although Roosevelt thought that contemporary Western civilization would probably not succumb to these evils because it was more widely dispersed than Rome, "the diminishing rate of increase of the population" loomed as the worldwide "feature fraught with most evil." New England and France continued to lose potency while the rate of increase also seemed to have slowed in Germany, England, and the southern United States. Sometime in the twentieth century,

5. TR, review of *Social Evolution* by Benjamin Kidd, in *Works*, XIV, 111, 128.
6. TR to Cecil Arthur Spring-Rice, August 5, 1896, in *Letters*, I, 554.

Roosevelt prophesied, the English-speaking peoples would probably reach Pearson's stationary state. The Russians, he noted uneasily, "as yet show no signs of this tendency, and though they may show it, and doubtless will in the next century, it certainly seems as if they would beat us in warfare of the cradle." If the bulk of American population reached the stationary state, Roosevelt argued, it could mean some "permanent deterioration" of the race stock. The solution to the problem could not be found in "extreme fecundity," which did not "guarantee social greatness," as the south Italians demonstrated with "the most fecund and the least desirable population of Europe." The correct response to the racial threat would be steady, fruitful procreation by the better classes.[7]

Roosevelt's preoccupation with the entire issue of race suicide continued as he returned to Washington in 1897 to become assistant secretary of the navy. In an era when racial theorizing was extremely popular, he rarely failed to utilize a public forum to decry the diminution of the breeding power of the race and often mentioned the matter in public and private correspondence. During the four years before he became president, TR gradually developed a morbid fascination with the specter of race suicide and assumed the self-appointed task of national exhorter for fertility, potency, and virility. Soon he raised the pitch of his exhortations to a strident level with a call for readers to join a moral crusade to save the nation and the race through the agency of healthy and vigorous reproductive activity. In the absence of appropriate public policy, the drift toward decadence seemed nearly irresistible.

Roosevelt feared that entire peoples including Americans lusted after ease and luxury, sought refinement, desired culture, and generally risked losing the rugged, virile virtues. To avoid decadence and to predominate, a race had to maintain the manly virtues; it had to work well, fight well, and breed well. If the American acquisition of effete characteristics continued unimpeded it could mean "the development of a cul-

7. TR to Cecil Arthur Spring-Rice, May 29, 1897, *ibid.*, I, 620–21.

tured and refined people quite unable to hold its own in those
conflicts through which alone any great race can ultimately
march to victory." Most ominously, however, the loss of the
"power of multiplying" threatened racial progress "so much
so as to make the fears of the disciples of Malthus a century
ago seem rather absurd to the dweller in France or New England today."[8] Although "the one ugly fact all over the world"
was the declining birthrate among the "higher races," Roosevelt continued to believe that the effects among the English-
speaking people did not yet merit sounding a full-scale alarm.
"I am confident," he wrote Spring-Rice in the late summer of
1897, "that as yet any decadence [among the English-speaking
peoples] is purely local."[9] Americans still increased at about
"twice the rate of the Russians" if one included immigrants.
Consequently, he felt that plenty of vigor remained in the stock
and that the vast majority of Americans had not yet become
effete like the "highly civilized" New Englanders. Even American presidents, he concluded, were probably not as effete as
"the average Czar or Russian minister."[10]

After the return from Cuba in 1898 and the encounter with
the Spanish, whom he believed were drifting into decadence,
Roosevelt seemed more convinced that a declining birthrate
among old-stock Americans did indeed offer a grave threat to
the nation as a whole. The next year Governor Roosevelt wrote
Spring-Rice that "evil forces" were working in America and
declared that "the diminishing birthrate among the old native
American stock, especially in the north east, with all that implies, I should consider the worst."[11] For this worst of all evils
Roosevelt offered the prescription of "Work—fight—breed." A
race could do all these things and still be "worthless"; but unless it did them, "it certainly *must* be worthless." Our race, he
told the anti-suffragist Helen Kendrick Johnson the same year

8. TR, review of *The Law of Civilization and Decay* by Brooks Adams, in *Works*
XIV, 135. See also TR to Granville S. Hall, November 29, 1899, in *Letters*, II, 110
9. TR to Cecil Arthur Spring-Rice, August 13, 1897, in *Letters*, I, 647.
10. *Ibid.*, 648.
11. TR to Cecil Arthur Spring-Rice, August 11, 1899, *ibid.*, II, 1053.

"is unfit to cumber the earth, if its men do not work hard . . .
and its women breed." [12]

To his sister Anna at Christmas time in 1899 Roosevelt confided his deepening fears: "I am an optimist but there are grave
signs of deterioration in the English-speaking peoples." Not
only was there an "evident lack of fighting edge" in the British soldiers then at war in South Africa, but also new and thoroughly alarming signs of a diminishing birthrate in England,
Canada, Australia, and the United States. These problems,
combined with the "excessive urban growth," "love of luxury,"
and "the turning of sport into a craze by the upper classes,"
posed formidable problems for the English-speaking race and
made prospects even worse. Moreover, these signs of decadence pointed to the possibility of an English defeat in South
Africa which would be a "race humiliation" and a "great catastrophe." [13]

By the time Roosevelt left the governor's chair in Albany to
return to Washington as vice-president, he had a fully developed theory of race suicide. Evidence of declining birthrates
in many of the Western nations and particularly among the
English-speaking peoples indicated that a two-fold threat existed. If the trend were not arrested, higher races might commit "race suicide" and literally die out, leaving no trace of the
superior qualities which accounted for the present state of civilization and constituted the best hope for the future. The second possible consequence of racial reproductive failure would
be the frightening prospect that lower races such as Latin Americans, blacks, and East Europeans would swamp the higher orders in the "warfare of the cradle." Abroad, the fecund Russians, rivals in the imperialistic struggle, threatened American
interests; and at home the virile blacks with their reproductive
powers undiminished by the presence of the white man constituted a menace for the "old stock."

For the next twenty years Roosevelt developed his theory,

12. TR to Helen Kendrick Johnson, January 10, 1899, *ibid.*, II, 905.
13. TR to Anna Roosevelt Cowles, December 17, 1899, *ibid.*, II, 1112–13.

dressed it in the robes of morality and national interest, and gave it peculiarly Rooseveltian accessories. During the brief tenure as vice-president any doubts which he might have had about the seriousness of race suicide further receded into the distance. TR admitted to Spring-Rice that there was "grave cause for anxiety"[14] and to another friend and correspondent, Hugo Münsterberg, he disclosed the profound significance which he attached to the matter. "All the other problems before us in this country, important though they may be, are as nothing compared with the problem of the diminishing birth-rate and all that it implies."[15] Throughout the presidential years the idea became a forceful element in Roosevelt's ideology as he gave much attention to the questions of decadence and race suicide and often proposed avenues of escape for the threatened racial "stocks." The sheer bulk of Roosevelt's writing and speaking on the entire issue demonstrated that he considered race suicide of great importance to the survival of "white civilization."[16]

As president, Roosevelt tied to the theory of race suicide and his traditional racial concerns, opinions on motherhood, sex, birth control, and the new role which women sought. Frequently he used his position as moral and political leader to spread his opinions on all these issues, to exhort women to fulfill a special role as perpetuators of the race, and to encourage them toward even more plenteous reproduction. Roosevelt's interest in the racial role of women can be traced to his Harvard days. His undergraduate thesis of 1880 on "Practicability of Equalizing Men and Women Before the Law" presaged his later concern about women and feminism.[17] As vice-president he had applauded Hugo Münsterberg's article "American

14. TR to Cecil Arthur Spring-Rice, March 16, 1901, *ibid.*, III, 15.

15. TR to Hugo Münsterberg, June 3, 1901, *ibid.*, III, 86.

16. Roosevelt's emphasis on the importance of race suicide does not fit John Higham's assessment of the entire matter as a "minor national phobia." Higham, *Strangers in the Land: Patterns of American Nativism, 1860–1925* (New York, 1973), 147.

17. For an interpretation of Roosevelt's attitudes toward women, see Elaine L. Silverman, "Theodore Roosevelt and Women: The Inner Conflict of a President and Its Impact on His Ideology" (Ph.D. dissertation, UCLA, 1973).

Women: German Point of View" for its "criticism upon a certain failure to realize that for women (as indeed for men) the home in its widest and fullest sense should be the prime end of life."[18] In his remarks Roosevelt stressed the idea that woman as keeper of the family and preserver of the race deserved commendation for her social and racial functions: "The first requisite in a healthy race is that a woman should be willing and able to bear children just as the men must be willing and able to work and fight."[19] He thought neither task an easy one but the woman's function as a childbearer was "a great injustice of nature" since she belonged to the "weakest half of the human race." Nevertheless, duty demanded that she fulfill her function and that man from gratitude treat her as "an equal partner." Moreover, "the higher and nobler the race is, the more nearly the marriage relation becomes a partnership on equal terms—the equality, of course, consisting not in the performance of the same duties by the two parties, but in the admirable performance of utterly different duties . . . in mutual forbearance and respect."[20]

Roosevelt's conception of womanhood was a romantic middle- and upper-class view. That he could classify women primarily as breeders and yet glorify the feminine racial role bespoke an unfamiliarity with the lot of their existence. After reading a lengthy article which dealt with the lives of female factory workers, Roosevelt stressed publicly the attitudes of these working women toward reproduction as evidence that even the laboring class might be losing its reproductive instinct. A widely reprinted reply to the author represented his first attempt as president to lead public opinion on race suicide. There was, Roosevelt said, "a most melancholy side to it [the article],

18. TR to Hugo Münsterberg, June 3, 1901, in *Letters*, III, 86. Reverence for the home and for the family proceeded quite naturally from Roosevelt's frequently expressed pride in his own wife and six children, from the late-nineteenth-century glorification of family life and possibly, from Roosevelt's conception of himself as benign patriarch of both the family and the nation.

19. TR to Hugo Münsterberg, June 3, 1901, *ibid.*, III, 86. See also Münsterberg's article "American Women: German Point of View," *International*, III (June, 1901), 607–33.

20. TR to Helen Kendrick Johnson, January 10, 1899, in *Letters*, II, 904–905.

when you touch upon what is fundamentally infinitely more important than any other question in this country—that is, the question of race suicide, complete or partial, which must follow from the attitude of our people as a whole toward wifehood, motherhood and fatherhood, if the feeling that you describe among the girls you met in the factory is typical of the class generally—for that is the numerically dominant class."

Before publication of the letter, Roosevelt asked the author, Mrs. Bessie Van Vorst, to omit the direct reference to the "girls" of the factory worker "class." While he apparently wished to avoid such direct references for political reasons, the implication that these representatives of the "numerically dominant class" might be drifting away from traditional attitudes toward parenthood seemed profoundly disturbing. He discharged his concern through a sternly worded sermon on the duties and glories of race maintenance. For those "denied" through no fault of their own the "highest of all joys which spring only from home life, from the having and bringing up of many healthy children," Roosevelt had "deep and respectful sympathy," much like "the sympathy one extends to the gallant fellow killed at the beginning of a campaign, or the man who toils hard and is brought to ruin by the fault of others." For those who consciously chose not to have children and thus avoided responsibility for maintaining the race stock, Roosevelt expressed scorn and severe criticism: "The man or woman who deliberately avoids marriage and has a heart so cold as to know no passion and a brain so shallow and selfish as to dislike having children, is in effect a criminal against the race and should be an object of contemptuous abhorrence by all healthy people."

These "race criminals" represented decadence and "corruption" already evident in the nation. When American men were not "anxious" to father children and women refused to "recognize that the greatest thing for any woman is to be a good wife and mother," the country had real cause for alarm. While the blame for this sexual lassitude could not be traced to "physical trouble," it could be found in the faulty character and the love of luxury and ease among both the upper class and the laboring class.[21]

Roosevelt easily negotiated the short leap from condemning childless women as racial "traitors" to determining the worth of a female as an American citizen by counting her children. Although admitting that he felt "a little shy about talking of the deepest things," he declared that "the pangs of childbirth make all men the debtors of all women." The mother, he added, had "a touch of a saint—that is, of course if she has the right spirit in her at all." Hamlin Garland's suggestion that multiple childbearing could destroy women physically did not impress Roosevelt, who replied that while he did not wish "to see a woman worn down and perhaps killed by too much maternity" his comparison of woman's role to that of a soldier still applied. "If the women flinch from breeding," he argued, "the deserved death of the race takes place even quicker." Like the soldier who fled in the face of enemy fire, the woman who "flinched" at having children earned Roosevelt's everlasting contempt and opprobrium.[22]

Roosevelt briefly considered the possibility that his attempts to arouse public opinion on race suicide lay outside the proper bounds of presidential affairs.[23] Characteristically, however, he resolved the matter in his own favor and continued the fight against "willful sterility" with a great variety of White House political weapons. One representative approach was to grant special recognition to some superior feat of breeding. "Three cheers for Mr. and Mrs. Bower and their really satisfactory American family of twelve children," he wrote upon receiving a photograph of the Bower aggregation. "That is what I call being good citizens," the president proclaimed.[24] On other occasions he effectively used the presidency as a platform from which to sanctify the institution of motherhood. For example,

21. TR to Mrs. Bessie Van Vorst, October 18, 1902, *ibid.*, III, 355–56.
22. TR to Hamlin Garland, July 19, 1903, *ibid.*, III, 520–21.
23. TR to Lawrence F. Abbott, July 8, 1907, *ibid.*, V, 707.
24. TR to Mr. and Mrs. R. T. Bower, February 14, 1903, *ibid.*, III, 425.

in 1905 he took his anti-race-suicide views to the National
Congress of Mothers with a speech in praise of all the familiar
"womanly" virtues and a conclusion which surely contributed
one of the most effusive encomiums to mothers in history:

> And as for the mother, her very name stands for loving unselfish-
> ness and self-abnegation, and, in any society fit to exist, is fraught
> with associations which render it holy.
>
> The woman's task is not easy—no task worth doing is easy—
> but in doing it, and when she has done it, there shall come to her
> the highest and holiest joy known to mankind; and having done
> it, she shall have the reward prophesied in Scripture; for her hus-
> band and her children, yes, and all people who realize that her
> work lies at the foundation of all national happiness and great-
> ness, shall rise up and call her blessed.[25]

Later in the year Roosevelt spoke to the Society of Friendly
Sons of St. Patrick in New York and read a telegram announc-
ing the birth of a grandson to one of the delegates. Roosevelt
congratulated the absent mother and jovially noted that the
telegram had been given to him "as a sop to certain of my well-
known prejudices."[26]

Sometimes Roosevelt used political action in an attempt to
put his theories into practice. For example, in his Sixth Annual Message in 1906 he asked the Congress to begin work on
a constitutional amendment which would place "the whole
question of marriage and divorce" under federal authority in
order to safeguard the nation's home life. Although the president was vague about the provisions of the proposed amendment, he apparently intended to promote childbearing by
restricting divorce and by strengthening the institution of marriage. In effect Roosevelt seemed to suggest that it was necessary to legislate fecundity! He told the Congress that "when
home ties are loosened; when men and women cease to regard
a worthy family life, with all its duties full performed, and all

25. TR, "The Woman and the Home," address before the National Congress of
Mothers, Washington, D.C., March 13, 1905, in *Works*, XVIII, 233.
26. Address at the dinner of the Society of Friendly Sons of St. Patrick, New York
City, March 17, 1905, in *Works*, XVIII, 45.

its responsibilities lived up to, as the life best worth living; then evil days for the commonwealth are at hand." In concluding the speech he noted, "there are regions in our land, and classes of our population, where the birth-rate has sunk below the death-rate" and he warned:

> Willful sterility is, from the standpoint of the nation, from the standpoint of the human race, the one sin for which the penalty is national death, race death; a sin for which there is no atonement; a sin which is the more dreadful exactly in proportion as the men and women guilty thereof are in other respects, in character, and bodily and mental powers, those whom for the sake of the State it would be well to see the fathers and mothers of many healthy children, well brought up in homes made happy by their presence.[27]

Roosevelt transparently referred, of course, to the old-stock American and to the "desirable" classes who were guilty of shirking their procreative duties. While his ardent acceptance of the doctrines of race suicide in itself is noteworthy, his serious contemplation of a constitutional amendment intended to point toward federally regulated and imposed birthrates is even more remarkable.

Although Roosevelt became the most forceful and articulate of race suicide propangandizers, his theories seemed wrongheaded to some race thinkers. In the view of a few eugenicists like Dr. John J. Cronin, Roosevelt's advocacy of increased breeding by old-stock Americans did not discriminate enough. Cronin argued against uncontrolled, unrestricted reproduction and declared that controlled population quality should be the goal. In an attempt to confront this objectionable notion and advance his own ideas of race suicide, President Roosevelt published a strongly worded condemnation of Cronin in the *Review of Reviews*. The physician, an advocate of health care for school children, had argued in another magazine that "a very little study of sociology will convince the advocates of the 'race suicide' idea that a few perfect children are

27. TR, *State Papers as Governor and President*, in *Works*, XVII, 442–43.

far better for the nation and for the family than a dozen unkempt degenerates, who add pathos to the struggle for existence, and who sink under the inflexible law of the survival of the fittest."[28]

Roosevelt in his article sought to discredit Dr. Cronin personally and to refute his ideas. While he conceded that the physician might not have been "consciously immoral," the president declared that it was "an unwarranted compliment to speak of his intellect as half-baked." Cronin had principally sinned, however, when he suggested that Americans should not automatically assume that they should increase the size of their families. Roosevelt, disturbed that someone would question the cardinal principle of his race suicide theories, responded that Cronin clearly had not taken the trouble to examine the vital statistics of states like Massachusetts which showed that "the average native American family of native American descent has so few children that the birth rate has fallen below the death rate." To Cronin's declaration that an increased incidence of physical defects was associated positively with larger families Roosevelt somewhat unscientifically replied that the physician had only to note that athletes were found most frequently in large families and that "in the ordinary family of but one or two children there is apt to be lower vitality than in a family of four or five or more." The critical issue, Roosevelt stressed, was "not between having a 'few perfect children'" and "'a dozen unkempt degenerates,'" but rather in producing enough children to perpetuate the race and the race stock.

Should any insensitive reader fail to discern that Roosevelt regarded race suicide as a grave threat, the president reiterated that the "greatest problem of civilization is to be found in the fact that well-to-do families tend to die out" and thus created "a tendency to the elimination instead of the survival of the fittest." That Roosevelt intended this message to reach a special audience became more apparent when he noted that the readers of the magazine in which he published the article did not generally include the "people with large families" but

28. Quoted in Morison (ed.), *Letters*, V, 636.

were "upper-class people who already tend to have too few children." TR claimed that arguments like Cronin's tended to give the upper classes "moral justification" for abortion and for every "unnatural prevention of childbearing." While many nations and "people in all countries" needed to be warned against "rabbit-like indifference" to large families, the average old-stock American and the "self-respecting son or daughter of immigrants" needed an even keener awareness of the perniciousness of small families. Race survival required four or more children, and parents who refused to conform to the president's version of family planning were "criminals"—and Dr. Cronin's article constituted "an incitement to such criminality."[29]

While Roosevelt bullied opponents of the idea, he also began to assess the potential threat of racial self-destruction upon the English-speaking race and upon the thrust of Western imperialism. He vowed, for example, to keep Hawaii for "the small, white landowners" and to "discourage by every method the race suicide which would be encouraged by the planters in their insistence upon bringing every kind of Asiatic to help them to make fortunes for a moment, and to insure the extinguishment of their blood in the future."[30] The president worried in particular about the threat of race suicide to Australia. If that nation failed to increase its rate of reproduction, "the yellow peril which they dread might be a very real peril for them indeed." To counter the threat Australians should "encourage in every way the kind of immigration they can assimilate and digest."[31] Still, he admitted the possibility of a "race conflict" in the Pacific and confided to Cecil Spring-Rice that Australia should prepare for such a contingency by accelerating the birthrate. While the inadequate American birthrate was call for alarm, he felt that an "ethnic conquest by a yellow race here on the mainland" could be prevented.[32]

Toward the end of the second presidential term Roosevelt

29. TR to Albert Shaw, April 3, 1907, *ibid.*, V, 636–38. The letter was published in the *Review of Reviews*, XXXV (May, 1907), 550–51.
30. TR to James Wilson, February 3, 1903, in *Letters*, III, 416.
31. TR to John St. Loe Strachey, September 8, 1907, *ibid.*, V, 787.
32. TR to Cecil Arthur Spring-Rice, December 21, 1907, *ibid.*, VI, 869.

focused once again on domestic implications of race suicide and expressed an even greater exasperation with the unwillingness of the "best people" to breed. To David Starr Jordan, president of Stanford University and leading eugenicist, he complained, "I feel pretty melancholy when I see how in this country, when there is no war to kill our bravest men, the best men nevertheless seem content [that] the citizens of the future come from the loins of others." [33] And as he prepared to surrender the presidency to William Howard Taft, he again revealed the extreme seriousness with which he regarded the threat of race suicide.

> Among the various legacies of trouble which I leave you there is none as to which I more earnestly hope for your thought and care than this. There are very big problems which we have to face in the United States. I do not know whether you yourself realize how rapid the decline in the birth rate is, how rapid the drift has been away from the country to the cities. In spite of our enormous immigration, there is a good reason to fear that unless the present tendencies are checked your children and mine will see the day when our population is stationary, and so far as the native stock is concerned is dying out.

No one man could do very much to arrest this trend, Roosevelt added, but he urged Taft to do as he had done and use the position of the presidency to argue against racial self-destruction.[34]

The fervor with which Roosevelt hawked the virtues of increased fertility for the better classes increased after he left the presidency. To the familiar calls for large families and the ceaseless invocations of women's racial duties he now added diatribes against birth control, family planning, and the "science" of eugenics. As Roosevelt grew older, he grew more pessimistic about the race's future and tended to emphasize even more strongly the moral responsibility of old-stock Americans to breed.

Before he mounted his final campaigns in America, how-

33. TR to David Starr Jordan, December 12, 1908, in Roosevelt Collection, Library of Congress.
34. TR to William Howard Taft, December 21, 1908, in *Letters*, VI, 1433–34.

ever, he preached the threat of decadence and racial death to several European audiences. On his way back to the United States from the African safari of 1910, Roosevelt stopped off at the Sorbonne, at Berlin, and at Oxford to deliver lectures. The fact that he devoted so large a portion of the Paris lecture to race decadence and suicide can be attributed to a special sense of mission toward a Gallic "race" plunging toward racial suicide. Roosevelt told the French scholars that he wished to discuss the "commonplace, every-day qualities and virtues," the most important of which was the duty to perpetuate the race. In the "great republics" like France and the United States willful sterility combined with the loss of virile virtues to pose a grave threat. The Frenchmen should remember that neither sophistication nor progress, neither "sensuous development of art and literature" nor "heaping up of sordid riches" could substitute for the loss of these "great fundamental virtues." The "chief of blessings" for any people "is that it shall leave its seed to inherit the land," he told the assemblage.[35]

Upon returning to the United States for another round of presidential politics, he resumed the domestic campaign and jumped into new national debate on eugenics. Always interested in measures and ideas which seemed to support his racial theories, he exchanged thoughts with Charles Benedict Davenport, Boston Brahmin, Harvard Ph.D., and director of the Eugenics Record Office at the Biological Laboratory of the Brooklyn Institute of Arts and Sciences.[36] Roosevelt agreed with Davenport that society could not permit "degenerates to reproduce their kind" and found it "really extraordinary that our people refuse to apply to human beings such elementary knowledge as every farmer is obliged to apply to his own stock breeding."

Any group of farmers who permitted their best stock not to breed, and let all the increase come from the worst stock, would be treated as fit inmates for an asylum. Yet we fail to understand that such

35. TR, "Citizenship in a Republic," in *Works*, XV, 356–58.
36. Solomon, *Ancestors and Immigrants: A Changing New England Tradition*, 148.

conduct is rational compared to the conduct of a nation which permits unlimited breeding from the worst stocks, physically and morally, while it encourages or connives at the cold selfishness or the twisted sentimentality as a result of which the men and women who ought to marry, and if married have large families[,] remain celibates or have no children or only one or two.

"Some day," Roosevelt told Davenport, "we will realize that the prime duty of the good citizen of the right type is to leave his or her blood behind him in the world, and that we have no business permitting the perpetuation of citizens of the wrong type."[37]

If Roosevelt agreed with several basic principles of the eugenics movement, he strenuously dissented from the ideas which contravened the race suicide dogma. Eugenicists generally believed that selective breeding was desirable and that this of necessity implied that large numbers of people would not reproduce themselves. Roosevelt favored extensive breeding from a somewhat larger gene pool and categorically rejected *any* measure which would not produce enough children to maintain racial integrity and national preeminence. To the "quality" argument of the eugenicists he replied that "when quantity falls off, thanks to willful sterility, the quality will go down too" and that quality mattered very little "if the quantity is so small that there is finally no product at all."[38]

Roosevelt attacked other fundamental axioms of eugenics in an article on "Twisted Eugenics" written for the *Outlook* in 1911. The focus of his objections, an earlier article entitled "Eugenics and Militarism," argued that wars resulted in the elimination of the best members of society and thus were antieugenic.[39] The former Rough Rider found the argument ridiculous and insisted that "militarism is an absolutely negligible factor from the standpoint of eugenics." To consider militarism as a danger to Americans was as ludicrous as considering "the

37. TR to Charles Benedict Davenport, January 3, 1913, in Roosevelt Collection, Library of Congress.
38. TR, "Race Decadence," *Outlook*, XCVII (April 8, 1911), 765; TR to Endicott Peabody, May 5, 1911, in *Letters*, VII, 258.
39. TR, "Twisted Eugenics," in *Works*, XIV, 167–78.

eating of horse-meat in honor of Odin as a danger to our spiritual life." Roosevelt thought it a "calamity for people of education and knowledge who understood what 'good breeding' means to tilt at windmills" and avoid the greater problem facing the nation.

Roosevelt also wished that the "wrong people could be prevented entirely from breeding." Regrettably, there was "as yet
. . . no way possible to devise [methods] which could prevent all undesirable people from breeding." Nevertheless, he felt that "criminals should be sterilized" and "feeble-minded persons forbidden to leave offspring behind them." In the absence of applied eugenics, however, "the emphasis should be placed" on getting "ordinary, everyday Americans" to breed.[40] "Let professors of eugenics turn their attention to making it plain to the average college graduates," he admonished, "that it is their prime duty to the race to leave their seed after them to inherit the earth."[41] If the best people failed to reproduce, Roosevelt warned, "the result must necessarily be race deterioration, unless the race is partly saved by the infusion into it of the blood of other races that have not lost the virile virtues."[42]

Perhaps he thought of some Latin Americans when he referred to "races" which had not lost the breeding habit. On a trip to South America in 1914 he investigated the birthrate there and found that North American performance compared unfavorably. Argentina, Chile, Uruguay, and Brazil could teach something to the English-speaking nations who seemed to have forgotten to "recognize and obey the primary laws of their racial being."[43] Upper-class South Americans had large families and Roosevelt found the women "charming and attractive" as well as "good, fertile mothers." Best of all, none of the "symptoms of that artificially self-produced dwindling of population" appeared there.[44] North Americans by comparison practiced the "capital sin of civilization" and did not understand as South

---

40. *Ibid.*, 170–72.
41. *Ibid.*, 175.
42. *Ibid.*, 178.
43. TR, *A Book-Lover's Holidays in the Open*, in *Works*, IV, 79.
44. *Ibid.*, 77.

Americans did that a man must "marry the woman he loves, as early as he can" so that the race might live. Without strenuous, frequent breeding the state would become "rotten at heart." To lose a "healthy, vigorous, natural sexual instinct is fatal," Roosevelt warned, "just as much so if the loss is by disuse and atrophy as if it is by abuse and perversion."[45]

The former chief executive rarely failed to take advantage of any forum providing even a remote opportunity to comment on the duty of Americans to be good breeders. Even a report on a hunting trip in the Canadian woods contained in *A Book Lover's Holidays in the Open*, afforded TR an opportunity to evangelize on race suicide. In a chapter entitled "A Curious Experience with a Moose," he related how as he watched his French Canadian hunting guides preparing supper the realization came that they offered "fine stuff out of which to make a nation," their race still being one of "primarily mothers and fathers." Thus inspired by the French Canadian sexual activity which had concerned him thirty years before, he returned to complaints about the "atrophy of a healthy sexual instinct" among Americans.[46]

The 1916 passage of the Sixteenth Amendment to the United States Constitution offered still another opportunity for Roosevelt to air his fears for the race's future. While the Congress prepared to enact tax legislation, Roosevelt lobbied against a feature of the proposed tax "so wrong that in principle it makes all other wrongs—and benefits—unimportant." The provision which offended the former president offered each family five-hundred-dollar tax exemptions for no more than two children: "This premium on race suicide" should be "stricken from the bill by the conscience of the nation" whether it resulted from "merely thoughtlessness, stupendous folly or bad intent." He believed the offending provision "deliberately" penalized families with more than two offspring. The legislation should provide exemptions for all children so as to encourage fecundity since the absence of such provisions meant "speedy racial ex-

45. *Ibid.*, 77–78.
46. *Ibid.*, 232–33.

tinction, speedy racial death." To avert the catastrophe, there
should be penalties in the form of higher taxes for individuals
and "pecuniary reward" for particularly heroic feats of childbearing. The "dullest public servant" should realize that natural law demanded that the average married couple have at
least three children and preferably four or more.[47]

With the fear growing that old-stock Americans had not ful-
filled their sexual duties, Roosevelt considered the possibility that the disease of race suicide might also be spreading to
newer "stocks." In 1911 his fears were confirmed when he discovered that second-generation Americans also had not been
breeding at a satisfactory rate. "This same racial crime is spreading almost as rapidly among the sons and daughters of immigrants as among the descendants of the native born," he observed in a review of Octavius Charles Beale's *Racial Decay*. If
the disease had affected members of the old stock, said Roosevelt, it would have been bad enough, but the immigrants' children had also contracted this affliction. The loss of virility
among the old stock had been due to "moral, and not physiological, shortcomings." For the immigrants as for the old stock,
he noted, "it is almost unnecessary to say that the sterility is
not physiological." The "true" cause of race suicide lay else-
where: "It is due to coldness, to selfishness, to love of ease, to
shrinking from risk, to an utter and pitiful failure in sense of
perspective and in power of weighing what really makes the
highest joy, and to a rooting out of the sense of duty or a twisting
of that sense into proper channels."[48] "Woe to the small souls
who shrink from facing the great adventure," he declaimed.
"Shame to those who choose to lead their lives in a round of
cheap self-indulgence and vapid excitement!"[49]

Roosevelt's last lengthy statement on race suicide came in
1917, less than two years before his death. A victim of prema-
ture aging, he may have unwittingly translated his own sense
of mortality into concern for the racial future of the American

47. TR, "A Premium on Race Suicide," *Outlook*, CV (September 27, 1913), 163–64.
48. TR, "Race Decadence," *Outlook*, XCVII (April 8, 1911), 764.
49. *Ibid.*, 767.

nation. In a remarkable article, occasioned doubtlessly by the birth control movement of the Progressive Era, Roosevelt departed markedly from several ideas which had characterized his race thinking for a lifetime. The fear of race suicide prompted most of these departures and revealed a Roosevelt who was no longer the absolute optimist but older and more pessimistic. Perhaps the greatest alteration in his thought related to his changing conception of what constituted an old-stock American. Now he included in this term (which he said he used with "elasticity") "all children of mothers and fathers born on this side of the water."[50] Yet even with the inclusion of these Americans, population statistics revealed a rapidly worsening situation in which parents averaged less than three children.

Roosevelt again placed considerable blame for the declining birthrate on the eugenicists and on "decadent" and "immoral" birth control "propagandists." While he agreed with eugenicists that the problem of securing "a relative increase of the valuable as compared with the less valuable or noxious elements in the population" could not be dealt with "unless we give full consideration to the universal influence of heredity," the Lamarckian TR emphasized that the "very great influence of environment" upon human development should not be forgotten. Evil could come "from permitting the unrestricted breeding" of the "feebleminded, utterly shiftless, and worthless," but he rejected out of hand the arguments of "extremists" who claimed that large families were generally undesirable from the woman's point of view and from society's perspective. Roosevelt wrote that these "propagandists" threatened the nation's future and represented "a pathological condition."[51] If America ignored birth control and eugenics propaganda then the race might be saved. If not, the nation might follow the example of France, a nation which could lose the 1918 war with Germany precisely because it had succumbed to the race sui-

50. TR, "Birth Reform from the Positive, Not the Negative Side," in *Works*, XXI, 161.
51. *Ibid.*, 162–64.

cide impulse. While he noted that the French were then performing heroically, their refusal to reproduce sufficient numbers to defend the country effectively had necessitated that they call for aid from "potent allies" to "hold back a foe" whom they had once been able to defeat "single-handed." Frenchmen had belatedly realized that one or two children per family meant "closely impending race suicide" and that "the man who leaves behind him no children" or only one son "must hereafter realize that he is not a patriot." If the American birthrate continued to decline as the French had, then America too would be "impotent in the face of powers like Germany, Russia, or Japan" and would be "passed by the great states of South America."[52]

In this valedictory on race suicide Roosevelt summarized his recommendations on how best to solve the problem. He overcame the repressions left over from his Victorian childhood to argue that men and women should be "eager lovers" anxious to fulfill their procreative functions. While individuals could solve the problem through increased sexual activity, the government must help by giving preference to families with three or more children "as regards all obligations to the state." In addition, the state could also keep salaries low for all childless public officials and show "a marked discrimination . . . in favor of the man or woman with a family of *over* three children." All taxes, including those on incomes and inheritances, should be "immensely heavier on the childless and on the families with one or two children." Moreover, Roosevelt proposed a five-hundred-dollar income tax exemption for each of the first two children and one thousand dollars for each subsequent child, while no exemptions should be allowed for single individuals or childless couples. In the end, however, the battle against race suicide could only be won through a "sterner sense of duty and a clear vision of the perspectives among which duty must work."[53]

Roosevelt's proposals to encourage a higher birthrate through

52. *Ibid.*, 165–66.
53. *Ibid.*, 168–69.

various legal compensations for those who did breed well and penalties for those who did not, indicate both the seriousness with which he regarded the phantom of race suicide and the fantastic extremes to which he would go in order to avert the imagined death of the race. While it is difficult to judge the impact of his race suicide exhortations on the public at large, a sampling of his incoming correspondence suggests that he had been heard and heeded in many parts of the country by people of various social stations. Consider, for example, the representative letter of Mrs. Fred Meyer of Chicago who asked Roosevelt to be the godfather of her new child. "Dear Ex-President," she wrote, "I had 7 boys born to me in eight years, all healthy and strong even if they come form [sic] a poor family with an income of 12 a week." Although the size of Mrs. Meyer's large family cannot be directly attributed to Roosevelt's rantings on race suicide, she clearly knew of TR's advocacy of large families and sought his approval. Certainly Roosevelt's race suicide and anti-birth-control efforts did little to improve the condition of women like Mrs. Meyer whose reproductive activity was interpreted as a mark of their worth as citizens and as members of the race.[54]

Roosevelt's race suicide theories were also received in the general context of boosterism by chambers of commerce which began to point pridefully to the birthrate as one more local asset. For example, the Downey-Marsh Valley Commercial Club of Downey, Idaho, boasted of the largest grain elevator in Idaho and also claimed to be "the center of the champion Anti-Race Suicide district in the United States—where the air is pure and the soil fertile, and health and happiness everyone's right." The club's secretary forwarded to Roosevelt a list of local families with over seven children and explained that listing those having five or more would have required too much space. During some months, he added, Downey Valley recorded "as many as fourteen births." In view of these facts and "knowing Roosevelt's well-known interest in large families," the club invited

54. Mrs. Fred Meyer to TR, March 26, 1912, in Roosevelt Collection, Library of Congress.

the former president to move to the "champion Anti-Race Suicide district of the United States."[55]

Roosevelt declined the invitation to remove to Idaho but he
remained a fervent, outspoken advocate of anti-race-suicide
measures until his death. Throughout his last years he explained
his acceptance of the notion of race suicide in theoretical terms
which emphasized his fears for the survival of the American
race stock. Yet the language of his appeals for a national and racial effort at procreation suggested that subtle psychological
forces were at work in his mind and that some of his appre-
hensions about race suicide could be interpreted as personal
fears. Much of the tone of that language was heavily sexual
and stressed potency, virility, and the need for a healthy and
vigorous sexual instinct. Particularly in two essays, "Race Decadence" and "Birth Reform from the Positive Not the Negative Side," Roosevelt revealed sexually charged thought. What
to conclude from this evidence is not absolutely clear, but it
seems plausible that an awareness of his own advancing age
and debilitated physical condition may have led him to translate personal physical concerns into an obsession about the
possible loss of national and racial potency. However that may
be, Theodore Roosevelt died making the extraordinarily inac-
curate prophecy of race suicide.

55. R. H. Doyle to TR, March 21, 1912, *ibid.*

Conclusion

Thus in the end the prospect of race suicide badly shook Roosevelt's confidence in the ability of the American "race" to absorb other races and to impart its dominant characteristics to future generations. The fears of the last years about race suicide contrasted sharply with the booming, belligerent optimism of his thought during most of his life. As a young man in the 1880s and the 1890s he had proclaimed the existence of a powerful and mighty American race which could triumph over all historical circumstances and all racial stocks. While he always continued in the assimilationist rhetoric to preach the potency and power of the American he simultaneously perceived the possibility of an impending racial disaster. The existence of these antithetical concepts in Roosevelt's mind produced a substantial amount of stress within his racial paradigm and ultimately threatened to fracture his basic explanation of human existence. However bizarre the race suicide notion may seem today, its effect on Roosevelt leaves no doubt as to the seriousness with which Progressive Era Americans regarded the idea of racial self-destruction and indeed the idea of race itself.

Roosevelt had broadly construed the idea of race to embrace a bevy of assumptions, concepts, and formal theories which permeated virtually every aspect of his thought. He saw race as the basic unit of human organization and used the concept to bring order, regularity, and consistency to his world view. As an instrument of historical analysis, race allowed for a simplistic view of the past absolutely reliant upon an understanding of racial differences, racial movements, and the Lamarckian principle of recapitulation. In addition, race functioned as a unifying theme for a social philosophy which awarded superior pedigrees and penalized inferior ones. A formal theory of race based on the best scientific thought of the day spawned an explanation of human experience which permitted the elevation of the white American to the level of Übermensch while concomitantly allowing for the debasement of nonwhites. The Lamarckian theory in particular could easily translate into a rationalization for the disparity between democratic ideals and the reality of a social situation more closely approximating the concept of "many men down" rather than the Rooseveltian rhetoric of "all men up." Stress upon the great breeding powers of the white American permitted the celebration of a process of racial and national assimilation which could only be endangered if the virile virtues were abandoned. In short, race acted as a unifying force in TR's mind.

In some respects Roosevelt's life itself was an acting out of the basic theoretical continuum which lay at the foundation of his racial thought. As a young historian, he vicariously experienced the barbarism of the "low-Dutch sea-thieves" with an enthusiasm which bordered on frenzy. His trips to the West where the virile virtues abounded were real-life pilgrimages in search of the "race-hardening" experience of the frontier, while the Cuban adventure represented an attempt to exercise the military virtues, key ingredients in the social efficiency which was the goal of every race. For Roosevelt the adjuration to "work, fight and breed" had special personal meaning. As governor, vice-president, and president, he followed a script which saw him cast as a character in whom reposed all the prime racial virtues—love of order, the ability to fight well, and even the ability to breed well. Similarly, as national and racial leader he eschewed all the enervating vices which could lead to racial decadence. Finally, toward the end of his life he became obsessed with notions of racial impotence, decadence, and death. While he sensed the power of the racial theme in his life, he regarded it as source of strength not debilitation. For Theodore Roosevelt race remained prime, the indivisible factor of human experience.

Bibliography

MANUSCRIPT COLLECTION

Library of Congress, Washington, D.C.
  Theodore Roosevelt Collection

BOOKS

Abbott, Lawrence F. *Impressions of Theodore Roosevelt*. Garden City, New York: Doubleday, 1919.

Bailey, Thomas A. *Theodore Roosevelt and the Japanese-American Crisis*. Stanford, Calif.: Stanford University Press, 1934.

Beale, Howard K. *Theodore Roosevelt and the Rise of America to World Power*. Baltimore: John Hopkins Press, 1956.

Bishop, Joseph Bucklin. *Theodore Roosevelt and His Time Shown in His Own Letters*. New York: C. Scribner's Sons, 1920.

Blum, John Morton. *The Republican Roosevelt*. Cambridge: Harvard University Press, 1954.

Burke, Kenneth. *The Philosophy of Literary Form: Studies in Symbolic Action*. Baton Rouge: Louisiana State University Press, 1941.

Burton, David H. *Theodore Roosevelt: Confident Imperialist*. Philadelphia: University of Pennsylvania Press, 1968.

Carney, Thomas F. *Content Analysis: A Technique for Systematic Inference from Communications*. Winnipeg: University of Manitoba Press, 1972.

Chessman, G. Wallace. *Theodore Roosevelt and the Politics of Power*. Boston: Little, Brown, and Company, 1969.

Curtin, Jeremiah. *The Mongols in Russia: A History*. Boston: Little, Brown, and Company, 1907.

Cutright, Paul Russell. *Theodore Roosevelt the Naturalist*. New York: C. Scribner's Sons, 1956.

Daniels, Roger. *The Politics of Prejudice: The Anti-Japanese Movement in California and the Struggle for Japanese Exclusion*. Berkeley: University of California Press, 1962.

Dennett, Tyler C. *John Hay*. New York: Dodd, Mead, and Company, 1934.

———. *Theodore Roosevelt and the Russo-Japanese War*. Gloucester: P. Smith, 1959.

Einstein, Lewis. *Roosevelt, His Mind in Action*. Boston and New York: Houghton Mifflin Company, 1930.

Esthus, Raymond A. *Theodore Roosevelt and the International Rivalries*. Waltham, Mass.: Ginn-Blaisdell, 1970.

———. *Theodore Roosevelt and Japan*. Seattle: University of Washington Press, 1967.

Fredrickson, George M. *The Black Image in the White Mind: The Debate on Afro-American Character and Destiny, 1817–1914*. New York: Harper and Row, 1971.

Gatewood, Willard B. *Theodore Roosevelt and the Art of Controversy: Episodes of the White House Years*. Baton Rouge: Louisiana State University Press, 1970.

Gossett, Thomas F. *Race: The History of an Idea in America*. New York: Schoncken Press, 1965.

Gwynn, Stephen, ed. *The Letters and Friendships of Sir Cecil Spring-Rice*. 2 vols. Boston: Houghton Mifflin Company, 1929.

Hagedorn, Hermann. *Roosevelt in the Badlands*. Boston: Houghton Mifflin Company, 1921.

———. *The Life of Theodore Roosevelt*. London: Harrap, 1919.

———, ed. *The Works of Theodore Roosevelt*. 24 vols. New York: C. Scribner's Sons, 1925.

Haller, John S., Jr. *Outcasts from Evolution: Scientific Attitudes of Racial Inferiority, 1859–1900*. Urbana: University of Illinois Press, 1971.

Haller, Mark H. *Eugenics: Hereditarian Attitudes in American Thought*. New Brunswick, New Jersey: Rutgers University Press, 1963.

Handlin, Oscar. *Race and Nationality in American Life*. Boston: Little, Brown, and Company, 1957.

Harbaugh, William Henry. *Power and Responsibility: The Life and Times of Theodore Roosevelt*. New York: Farrar, Straus, and Cudahy, 1961.

———, ed. *The Writings of Theodore Roosevelt*. Indianapolis and New York: Bobbs-Merrill, 1967.

Hart, Albert B., and H. R. Ferleger, eds. *Theodore Roosevelt Cyclopedia*. New York: Roosevelt Memorial Association, 1941.

Higham, John. *Strangers in the Land: Patterns of American Nativism, 1860–1925*. New York: Atheneum, 1973.

Hofstadter, Richard. *The American Political Tradition and the Men Who Made It*. New York: A. A. Knopf, 1948.

Jessup, Philip C. *Elihu Root*. 2 vols. New York: Dodd, Mead, and Company, 1938.

Johnson, Alex., ed. *The Life and Letters of Sir Harry Johnston*. London: J. Cape, 1929.

Jordan, Winthrop D. *White over Black: American Attitudes Toward the Negro, 1550–1812*. Chapel Hill: University of North Carolina Press, 1968.

Lane, Ann J. *The Brownsville Affair: National Crisis and Black Reaction*. Port Washington, New York: Kennikat Press, 1971.

Leary, John J., Jr. *Talks with Theodore Roosevelt*. Boston: Houghton Mifflin Company, 1920.

Lodge, Henry Cabot, ed. *Selections from the Correspondence of Theodore Roosevelt and Henry Cabot Lodge, 1884–1918*. 2 vols. New York: Da Capo Press, 1925.

Lorant, Stefan. *The Life and Times of Theodore Roosevelt*. New York: Doubleday, 1959.

Lovejoy, Arthur O. *Essays in the History of Ideas*. Baltimore: John Hopkins Press, 1948.

March, Francis A. *A Thesaurus Dictionary of the English Language*. Philadelphia: Historical Publishing Company, 1902.

Mathews, Mitford M. *A Dictionary of Americanisms on Historical Principles*. Chicago: University of Chicago Press, 1951.

Montagu, Ashley. *Man's Most Dangerous Myth: The Fallacy of Race*. New York: Oxford University Press, 1974.

Morison, Elting E., ed. *The Letters of Theodore Roosevelt*. 8 vols. Cambridge, Mass.: Harvard University Press, 1951.

Morris, Charles, ed. *Universal Dictionary of the English Language*. 4 vols. New York: Collier and Son, 1902.

Mowry, George E. *The Era of Theodore Roosevelt*. New York: Harper, 1958.

———. *Theodore Roosevelt and the Progressive Movement*. Madison: Hill and Wang, 1947.

Nash, Gary B., and Richard Weiss, eds. *The Great Fear: Race in the Mind of America*. New York: Holt, Rinehart and Winston, 1970.

Neu, Charles E. *An Uncertain Friendship: Theodore Roosevelt and Japan, 1906–1909*. Cambridge: Harvard University Press, 1967.

Newby, Idus A. *Jim Crow's Defense: Anti-Negro Thought in America, 1900–1930.* Baton Rouge: Louisiana State University Press, 1965.

Pringle, Henry F. *Theodore Roosevelt: A Biography.* New York: Harcourt, Brace, and Company, 1931.

Putnam, Carleton. *Theodore Roosevelt: The Formative Years.* New York: Scribner, 1958.

Roosevelt, Theodore. *African and European Addresses.* New York: C. Scribner's Sons, 1910.

———. *America and the World War.* New York: C. Scribner's Sons, 1915.

———. *Fear God and Take Your Own Part.* New York: George H. Doran, 1916.

———. *The Negro Question: Attitude of the Progressive Party Toward the Colored Race.* New York: Mail and Express Job Print, 1912.

———. *Realizable Ideals.* San Francisco: Whitaker and Ray and Wiggin, 1912.

———. *Theodore Roosevelt's Diaries of His Boyhood and Youth.* New York: Scribner, 1928.

Rudwick, Elliot M. *Race Riot at East St. Louis, July 2, 1917.* Carbondale: Southern Illinois University Press, 1964.

Shaler, Nathaniel S. *The Autobiography of Nathaniel Southgate Shaler.* New York: Houghton Mifflin Company, 1909.

Sinkler, George. *The Racial Attitudes of American Presidents from Abraham Lincoln to Theodore Roosevelt.* New York: Doubleday, 1971.

Solomon, Barbara. *Ancestors and Immigrants: A Changing New England Tradition.* Cambridge: Harvard University Press, 1956.

Stanton, William. *The Leopard's Spots: Scientific Attitudes Toward Race in America, 1815–1859.* Chicago: University of Chicago Press, 1960.

Stocking, George W. *Race, Culture, and Evolution: Essays in the History of Anthropology.* New York: Free Press, 1968.

Thayer, William Roscoe. *Theodore Roosevelt: An Intimate Biography.* Boston: Houghton Mifflin Company, 1919.

Thompson, Arthur W., and Robert A. Hart. *The Uncertain Crusade: America and the Russian Revolution of 1905.* Amherst, Mass.: University of Massachusetts Press, 1970.

Ullman, Stephen. *Semantics, the Science of Meaning.* London: B. Blackwell, 1967.

van den Berghe, Pierre L. *Race and Racism*. New York: Wiley, 1967.

Viereck, George Sylvester. *Roosevelt: A Study in Ambivalence*. New York: Jackson Press, 1920.

Wagenknecht, Edward. *The Seven Worlds of Theodore Roosevelt*. New York: Longmans, Green, and Company, 1958.

Weaver, John D. *The Brownsville Raid*. New York: W. W. Norton, 1970.

Wheelock, John Hall. *A Bibliography of Theodore Roosevelt*. New York, 1920.

White, G. Edward. *The Eastern Establishment and the Western Experience: The West of Frederic Remington, Theodore Roosevelt and Owen Wister*. New Haven: Yale University Press, 1968.

Wilhelm, Donald. *Theodore Roosevelt as an Undergraduate*. Boston: J. W. Luce, 1910.

Wise, Gene. *American Historical Explanations*. Homewood, Illinois: Dorsey Press, 1973.

Wister, Owen. *Roosevelt: The Story of a Friendship*. New York: The Macmillan Company, 1930.

ARTICLES

Cordingley, Nora E. "Extreme Rarities in the Published Works of Theodore Roosevelt." *Papers of the Bibliographical Society of America*, XXXIX (1945), 20–50.

Cronin, John J. "The Doctor in the Public School." *Review of Reviews*, XXXV (April, 1907), 433–40.

Crowe, Charles. "Tom Watson, Populists, and Blacks Reconsidered." *Journal of Negro History*, LV (1970), 99–116.

Grantham, Dewey W., Jr. "Theodore Roosevelt in American Historical Writing, 1945–1960." *Mid-America*, XLIII (1961), 3–35.

Guild, Curtis, Jr. "Theodore Roosevelt at Harvard." *Harvard Graduate Magazine*, X (1938), 177–83.

Hagan, William T. "Civil Service Commissioner Theodore Roosevelt and the Indian Rights Association." *Pacific Historical Review*, XLIV (1975), 187–200.

Kennan, George. "The Psychology of Mr. Roosevelt." *North American Review*, CCIII (1916), 790–94.

Laughlin, J. Laurence. "Roosevelt at Harvard." *Review of Reviews*, XXX (1924), 512–14.

Merriam, Clinton Hart. "Suggestions for a New Method of Discriminating Between Species and Subspecies." *Science*, V (May 14, 1897), 753–58.

Robinson, Elwyn B. "Theodore Roosevelt: Amateur Historian." *North Dakota History*, XXV (1958), 5–13.

Roosevelt, Theodore. "Brazil and the Negro." *Outlook*, CVI (February 21, 1914), 409–11.

———. "Buenos Aires: A Fine Modern Capital." *Outlook*, CVI (March 28, 1914), 696–713.

———. "A Layman's Views on Specific Nomenclature." *Science*, V (April 30, 1897), 685–88.

———. "Letter from President Roosevelt on Race Suicide." *Review of Reviews*, XXXV (May, 1907), 550–51.

———. "Lynching and the Miscarriage of Justice." *Outlook*, XCIX (November 25, 1911), 706–707.

———. "Negro in America." *Outlook*, XCV (June 4, 1910), 241–44.

———. "Premium on Race Suicide." *Outlook*, CV (September 27, 1913), 163–64.

———. "The Progressives and the Colored Man." *Outlook*, CI (August 24, 1912), 909–12.

———. "Race Decadence." *Outlook*, XCVII (April 8, 1911), 763–69.

Scheiner, Seth M. "President Theodore Roosevelt and the Negro, 1901–1908." *Journal of Negro History*, XLVII (July, 1962), 169–82.

Sellen, Robert W. "Theodore Roosevelt: Historian with a Moral." *Mid-America*, XLI (1959), 223–40.

Small, Melvin. "Some Suggestions from the Behavioral Sciences for Historians Interested in the Study of Attitudes." *Societas*, III (Winter, 1973), 1–19.

Tinsley, James A. "Roosevelt, Foraker, and the Brownsville Affair." *Journal of Negro History*, XLI (1956), 43–65.

Trent, W. P. "Theodore Roosevelt as an Historian." *Forum*, XXI (1896), 566–76.

Turner, F. J. Reviews of *The Winning of the West*, by Theodore Roosevelt. *The Dial*, X (1889), 71–73; *The Nation*, LX (1892), 240–42; *The Nation*, LXIII (1895), 277; *American Historical Review*, II (1896), 171–76.

UNPUBLISHED WORKS

Haney, James. "Theodore Roosevelt and Afro-Americans, 1901–1912." Ph.D. dissertation, Kent State University, 1971.

Silverman, Elaine Leslau. "Theodore Roosevelt and Women: The Inner Conflict of a President and Its Impact on His Ideology." Ph.D. dissertation, University of California, 1973.

Index

Aborigines, 75
Adams, Brooks, 125
Adams, Henry, 10, 45
Adams, Herbert Baxter, 46
Africans, 117–18
Aguinaldo, Emilio, 140
American Historical Association, 131
Americanization: assimilation, 132–33; and hyphenation, 133–34; groups excluded, 134–42
American "race": formation and distinctiveness of, 49, 51, 62–63, 131–32; ability for self-government, 53; mentioned, 29, 64, 65, 142, 143
Americans: branch of English race, 48–49; race history, 57–59; as soldiers, 136; as guardians of civilization, 141
Ancestors and Immigrants, 143
Anderson, Charles W., 99
Anglo-conformity, 133
Anglo-Saxonism, 1, 5–6, 8, 9, 17, 26, 27, 29, 47, 53, 64–65, 67
Anthropology, 41, 143
Anti-Catholicism, 125–29
Anti-Semitism, 124–25
Arabs, 4, 71
Aryan, 17, 26, 28, 67, 136
Assimilation: of blacks, 119–21; of immigrants, 129–34; mentioned, 84, 144
Atlanta *Constitution*, 108
Australia, 62, 157
Australians, 28, 58

Backward races, 109–10, 116, 140–41
"Backwoods race," 28
Balfour, Arthur J., 13
Battle of New Orleans, 49
Beale, Octavius C., 163

Benton, Thomas Hart, 50, 131
Berlin, University of, 19
Bijur, Nathan, 124
"Biological Analogies in History," 16, 33–37
Birth control, 150, 164
Blacks: as TR's servants, 4, 5; lynching, 7, 112–14; as backward race, 16, 109–10, 116; as soldiers, 50, 100–101; intermixture with whites, 84, 118–22; as children, 90; inferiority of, 90–91, 95, 97–98, 106, 109, 120, 121; and evolution, 91, 92, 97, 100, 105, 110, 122; and Lamarckianism, 92; historical image, 93–96; fecundity, 95; political participation, 96–109; as office holders, 98–105, 107–108; in Spanish-American War, 100–101; privileged, 103, 104, 105, 109; sexual exploitation, 107; social control of, 109–16; unfit for suffrage, 109; and education, 110–11; and crime, 111–14; and race solidarity, 112–13, 114; African, 117–18; Latin American, 118–21; Brazilian, 119–21; unqualified for assimilation, 134; and race suicide, 149
Blaine, James G., 96
"Blood," 24–25, 38, 42, 56, 61
Boas, Franz, 18
Boer War, 149
Bolin, Gaius W., 99
Boxer Rebellion, 136
Brazilians, 118–21
British, the, 28, 48
Brownsville (Texas), incident, 114–16
Burgess, John, 7–8, 9

Cable, George W., 98

Caesar, 58
Canadians, 62
Caractacus, 58
Carroll, Charles, xiii, 13, 92
Catholics, 125–29
Celts, 56, 61, 63, 64
A Century of Dishonor, 80
Chamberlain, Houston Stewart, xiii, 13
Characteristics, acquired, 37, 40, 43
Chinese, 14, 15, 139–40
Chivington, J. M., 79
Civilis the Batavian, 58
Cleveland, Grover, 103
Clovis, 58
Colombians, 140
Columbia University, 7, 8, 20
Cooley, Charles H., 23
Cooper, James Fenimore, 2
Cornplanter, 74
Cowles, Anna Roosevelt, 125, 149
Cox, Minnie M., and Indianola affair,
    102–103
Craniology, 15–16, 17
Creoles, 49–50, 118
Cronin, John J., 155–56
Crum, William, 102, 103–104, 107, 109
Cubans, 141

Danish, the, 56
Darwin, Charles, 1, 31, 91
Darwinism, 5, 8, 9, 13, 52
Davenport, Charles B., 14, 159
Decadence, 13
Decadence, racial, 13, 36–37, 42, 147,
    148, 150, 152, 159
Demolin, Edmond, 12
Demosthenes, 74
Dewey, John, 19
Divorce, 154
Dixon, Roland B., 18
Dohrn, Anton, 13
Dreisch, Hans, 13
Dunbar, Paul, 102
Durbin, Winfield T., 114
Dutch, the, 28, 30, 48, 132
Dutch "race," 37

Education, 110–11
English, expansion to America, 59
English, the: and linguistic ascendancy,
    60; intermarriage with Indians, 84;
    mentioned, 32
English "race," 48, 49, 57, 62–63

English-speaking peoples: spread of,
    55; race-history of, 58; and "stationary-
    state," 147; deterioration of, 149; men-
    tioned, 12
English-speaking race: defined, 28–29;
    and race suicide, 144, 149, 157; men-
    tioned, 1, 68, 142
Environment: and Lamarckianism, 38–
    39, 43; in formation of American race,
    43, 51; mentioned, 7, 13
Epstein, Edwin, 124
Equipotentiality (of races), 39, 40, 92,
    100, 105
Eugenics, 144, 155–56, 158, 159, 160–
    61, 164
Eugenics Record Office, 14, 159
Europeans, East, 149
Evansville, Indiana, race riot (1903), 114
Evolution: effect on TR's racial theory,
    31–44; unilinear, 40–41, 43; and
    blacks, 105, 106; mentioned, 1, 141

Family, the, 12, 151, 163, 165
Fascism, 13
Fellow-feeling, 23
Fifteenth Amendment, 106
Filipinos, 140–41
Finot, Jean, 13
Fisk University, 111
Foraker, James, 115
Fortune, T. Thomas, 99–100
Forum, 133
Franks, the, 56
Freeman, Edward A., 45
French, the: bastardy of, 58; and In-
    dians, 75, 76; threatened by race sui-
    cide, 146, 164–65; and race suicide,
    159; mentioned, 64
French Canadians: and race suicide,
    144, 162; mentioned, 29
French "race," 28, 29, 54
Froebel, Friedrich, 30
Frontier, the, 65–67
Frontiersman, American: parallel with
    Siegfried, 3; compared to Viking, 51;
    as racial type, 54; ethnic composition
    of, 65–66; mentioned, 41

Gaffney, Thomas St. John, 27
Galton, Francis, 90
Garland, Hamlin, 153
Gatewood, Willard, 104
Gauls, the, 56

Genealogy, 9
"Gentlemen's Agreement" (1907), 138
Germanic peoples: expansion of, 55–58; racial purity of, 58
German "race," 29, 56, 62–63
Germans, the, 30, 32, 57, 127, 132, 146, 165
Gobineau, Arthur de, xiii, 90
Gouverneur Morris, 47, 54
Grant, Madison, xiii, 13, 17, 92
Greeks, 62

Haeckel, Ernst, 39
Haiti, 48, 109
Half-breeds, 75
Harbaugh, William, xii, xiii
Hardraada, Harold, 52
Harrison, Benjamin, 102–103
Harvard College, 5–7, 8, 20
Hawaii, 135, 141, 157
Hemenway, James A., 116
Hengist, 58
Heredity, 13, 38, 43, 46
Herrick, Francis H., 39
"Higher races," 36, 148
Hispano-Indian race, 30n
Historians, 45
Hitchcock, Ethan A., 85
Hitler, Adolf, xiii
Horsa, 58
Houston, Sam, 52
Howell, Clark, 108
Huguenots, 63
Hunting Trips of a Ranchman, 9
Hyphenation, 133–34

Immigration, restriction of, 14, 129–30, 135, 137
Imperialism, 10, 12, 139–42, 157
Incas, the, 61
Indian Rights Association, 82
"Indianola affair," 102–103
Indians: foes of whites, 62; as savages, 70, 71–72, 74; tribes, 70–71, 73, 78–79, 86; cruelty of, 71–72; penchant for liquor, 72–73; 83; and Christianity, 73; massacre of, 73, 79; as noble savages, 74; as orators, 74; rationale for displacement, 74–81; and expansion of frontier, 75; Canadian, 75; as fighters, 75, 76; "race-importance" of conflict with, 76; conquest of, 78; grievances rationalized, 78–80; policy of U.S. government, 78–81; indemnification of, 79; righteousness of warfare with, 79; ownership of land, 80–81, 84–85; adaptation of white ways, 81, 83, 88; reservation policy toward, 81; as Rough Riders, 82; education, 83; intermarriage with whites, 83–84; rights of, 84; and stages-of-development scheme, 85; punishment of, 85–86; TR's positive assessment of culture, 86–87; mentioned, 8, 50, 64
Indian Service, corruption of, 82, 85
The Inequality of Human Races, 90
Inferior races, 60–61, 146
Intermixture, racial, 59, 60, 118–21, 132, 138. *See also* Miscegenation
Irish, the, 27, 30, 49, 63, 65, 125–27, 129, 132
Italians, 30, 32, 37, 50, 135, 147

Jackson, Helen H., 80
James, William, 19
Japanese: TR admires racial qualities, 136–37; and immigration, 135–39; and race suicide, 165; mentioned, 30
Jefferson, Thomas, 74
Jewish "race," 17, 125
Jews, 32, 124–25
"Jim Crow" laws, 89–90, 102
Johnson, Helen K., 148
Jordan, David S., 14, 158

Kentucky "race," 28
Kentuckian, as racial type, 7, 66
Kidd, Benjamin, 31–32
Kipling, Rudyard, xiii, 12, 140
Kiskinev Massacre (1903), 124
Know-Nothing movement, 128
Knox, Philander, 113, 138

Lady Baltimore, 106, 106n
Lamarckianism: TR's acceptance of, 6, 7; importance in TR's racial theory, 37–44; related to Anglo-Saxonism and Teutonism, 46; and Blacks, 92, 97–98, 106, 110; and Jewish "race," 125; and race suicide, 164; mentioned, 8, 17, 169
Language: related to racial superiority, 6; TR's usage in racial context, 21–30; mentioned, 58, 59, 60, 62
Latin Americans: TR observes, 117–21; and imperialism, 140–42; unqualified

for assimilation, 134–35; and race sui-
cide, 149, 161, 165; mentioned, 30
Latin "race," 28, 29, 52, 58, 76
LeBon, Gustave, 11, 980
Lewis, William H., 101–102
Lodge, Henry Cabot, 10–11, 12, 16, 96,
109, 129
Logan, Chief, 74
Longfellow, Henry W., 2
L'Origine degli Indo-Europei, 67
Low-Dutch sea-thieves, 51, 57, 58, 59,
62, 64, 169
Lynch, John R., 96–97
Lynching, 7, 90, 102, 112–14

McKinley, William, 102, 103
McKittrick, Hugh, 99
McMaster, John B., 45
Mahan, Alfred T., 10, 12, 141
Malthus, Thomas, 148
Manypenny, George W., 80
Maoris, 62, 76
Mathews, James B., 18
The Medieval Mind, 27
Mediterranean race, 13, 120
"Melting-pot" theory, 130–31
Merrian, C. Hart, 24
Mexicans, 52–53, 61
Meyer, Mrs. Fred, 166
Michelis, E. de, 13, 67
Miscegenation, 91, 107, 118–21, 138
Montessori, Maria, 30
Montezuma, 61
Moravians, 73
Morris, Gouverneur, 54
Mulatto, 30, 121
Münsterberg, Hugo, 150

National Congress of Mothers, 154
National Life and Character, 11, 144
Nations, formation of, 36
Nativism, 123–27, 129–31, 131–40. *See
also* Immigration
Natural selection, 1, 32, 33, 39
The Naval War of 1812, 9, 27, 46, 47, 50,
53
The Negro a Beast, 13
Neo-Lamarckianism, 37, 38, 39, 40–44.
See also Lamarckianism
Nibelungenlied, 2, 3, 3n
No Shirt, Chief, 85
Nordicism, 2, 36, 47, 51

Norsemen, 49
Northern races, 35
Northwest, settlement, 63
Norwegians, 56
Nott, Josiah, 90

Odin, 55
"Old-stock" Americans, 130, 143–44,
145
The Origin and Evolution of Life, 14, 40
*The Origin and Growth of Moral In-
stinct*, 15
Orientals, 14, 84, 134–35, 142, 157
Osborn, Henry F., 14, 16, 19, 33, 35, 40
Our Indian Wards, 80
Our Young Folks, 3–4
Outlook, 119, 160
Oxford University, 16, 19, 33

Paleontology, 16
Pan American Exposition Board, 99
Parkman, Francis, 8, 9, 46–47, 77–78,
144
The Passing of the Great Race, 17
Pearson, Charles, 11, 144
Persians, 136
Peruvians, 61
Physiognomy, 41
Poles, 32
*Political Science and Comparative Con-
stitutional Law*, 7
Portuguese, the, 50, 135
Preparedness, 134
Presbyterian Irish, the, 28, 66, 127
Progress, idea of, 32, 33, 39
Progressive party, 109
Pseudoscience, 90

Race: concept of, 10–11, 13–14, 17, 21–
30; and history, 16; language of, 21–
30; and culture, 26, 38, 41–42, 137–
38; and natural history, 34–37
Race, Culture, and Evolution, 37
Race Prejudice, 14
Race purity, 57–59
Race suicide: fear of immigrants, 143–
44; and French Canadians, 144; and
higher races, 145; and Russians, 148,
149; and blacks, 149, and East Europeans, 149; and Latin Americans, 149,
161–62; and women, 150–54; and
federal legislation, 154–55; and impe-

rialism, 157; and eugenics, 159–60; and taxation, 162–63; 165; among immigrants, 163; mentioned, 12, 15, 17, 121, 130

The Racial Attitudes of American Presidents from Abraham Lincoln to Theodore Roosevelt, 28

Racial Decay, 163

Ranch Life and the Hunting Trail, 71

Recapitulation, 48–49, 59, 63

Reinsch, Paul, 38

Republican National Convention (1884), 96

Republican party, 89

Republicans, 103, 104

Review of Reviews, 14

Rhett, Robert G., 107–108

Rhodes, James F., 14, 45

Ridgeway, William, 13, 41

Romanes lecture, 16, 33

Romantic race, 30*n*

Rome, 37, 146

Roosevelt, Alice Lee, 8

Roosevelt, Martha Bulloch, 5, 8

Roosevelt, Theodore: scholarly assessment of, xii–xiii; origins of racial thought, 2–5; education, formal, 2, 5–8; childhood journey to Mid-East, 4; southern heritage, 5, 93–94; as state legislator, 8, 126; as Civil Service Commissioner, 9, 81–82, 86, 98–99, 128; as governor of New York, 12, 82, 99; as vice-president, 12, 101; racial interests as president, 12–14; and social science, 14; as scholar, 18; as zoologist, 18–19; African trip (1909), 33; as historian, 46–47; journeys to West, 76, 77; rationalizes Indian grievances, 78–80; and reform in Indian affairs, 82; Indian policy as president, 83–87; visits Sioux reservation, 84; as "father" to Indians, 85; softening of attitude toward Indians, 86–88; visits Navajo and Hopi, 87; as racial moderate, 92; contacts with blacks as youth, 93; and slavery, 94–96; 1884 Republican convention, 96–97; criticizes suffrage restriction, 98; patronage policy for blacks, 99–100, 108; criticizes black soldiers in Cuba, 100–101; 1904 election of, 103; attitude toward southerners, 107; unsuccessful as president with racial problems, 107; Brownsville incident (1906), 114–16; travels in Africa and South America, 117–22; anti-Irish views, 126–27; exploits immigration controversy, 130; Japanese question as president, 138–39; lecture at Sorbonne and Berlin, 159

Ross, Edward A., 14–15, 16

Rough Riders, the, 82

Russians, 136, 165

Saga of King Olaf, 2

Sand Creek Massacre, 79

Sapir, Edward, 22

Savagism, 70

Scandinavians, 63

The Science and Philosophy of the Organism, 13

Scotch-Irish, the, 28, 65. *See also* Presbyterian Irish

Scots, 132

Scribner's Magazine, 100

Self-government, instinct for, 53, 54

Sergi, Giuseppe, 13

Sewanee Review, 11

Sexual misconduct: by Japanese, 139; by blacks, 113–14

Shaler, Nathaniel S., 6–7, 9

Shaw, Albert, 14

Sheridan, Philip, 128

Sherman, William T., 128

Siegfried, 3

Simmons, Harvey L., 111

Sinkler, George, xiii, 28

Sixteenth Amendment, 162

Skull types, 41

Slavic race, 30*n*

Slavonians, 136

Slavs, 135, 136

Social Control, 15

Social efficiency, 42, 141

Social equality, 92, 108–109

Social Evolution, 31

Society of Friendly Sons of St. Patrick, 154

Sociology, 143

Solidarity, racial, 112–13

Solomon, Barbara, 143

Sorbonne, the, 19

South Africa, 61

South Africans, 28

Southwest, settlement, 63

Southwesterner, as racial type, 63–65
Spanish, the: bastardy of, 58; conquests of, 60–61; and Indians, 76; mentioned, 12, 28, 64, 135
Spanish-American War, 82, 100–101
Spring-Rice, Cecil A., 12, 16, 135, 136, 146, 148, 150, 157
Stages of development, 42–43
Stanford University, 14
Stereotypes, 49, 124–25
Sterilization, 161
Stocking, George, 37–38
Straus, Oscar, 124
Stubbs, William, 45
Sumner, William Graham, 8
Supériorité des Anglo-Saxons, 12
"Survival of the fittest," 1, 156
Sutherland, Alexander, 15
Syagrius, 58

Taft, William H., 138, 158
Taxation, and race suicide, 162–63, 165
Taylor, Henry Osborne, 27
Tecumseh, 27
Tennessee, settlement of, 65
Teutonism, 2, 3, 5, 8, 9, 10, 17, 29, 36, 45, 46–51, 53, 57, 65, 66–67
Texas, conquest of, 52
Texas "race," 28
Thomas Hart Benton, 47, 50, 51, 53
Tillman, Benjamin R., 92
Tourgée, Albion, 105, 105n
Trevelyan, George O., 12
Turner, Frederick J., 18, 54
Tyler, Moses C., 45
Types of Mankind, 90

Übermensch, 169
Uplift, for blacks, 110–11

van denk Berghe, Pierre L., xiii
Van Vorst, Bessie, 152
Vardaman, James K., 92, 103
Varus, 55
Vercingetorix, 58
Vespasian, 58
Vikings, 51
The Virginian, 106
Virtues, virile, 42, 43–44, 147, 161
Von Sternberg, Herman Speck, 135

Wald, 55
Walker, Francis A., 8
Walsh, James J., 33
War of 1812, pp. 47–50
Washington, Booker T., 102, 105
Watson, Thomas E., 92, 128
Weismann, August, 39, 90–91
Welsh, the, 48
Welsh, Herbert, 82
Wheeler, Benjamin I., 14, 67
White "race," 76, 83–84, 95–97
The Winning of the West, 3, 9, 31, 46, 47, 54, 55, 73, 81, 84, 94, 119
Wister, Owen, 106, 107
Women: and race suicide, 150–54, 164–66; TR's view of, 151–54
World War I, 133

"Yellow peril," 139, 157

Zangwill, Israel, 131
Zulus, 62, 77